Drinking
and
Tweeting

Drinking
and
Tweeting

– and other **brandi blunders** –

BRANDI **GLANVILLE**

with Leslie Bruce

GALLERY BOOKS

New York   London   Toronto   Sydney   New Delhi

G

Gallery Books
A Division of Simon & Schuster, Inc.
1230 Avenue of the Americas
New York, NY 10020

First Gallery Books trade paperback edition January 2014

GALLERY BOOKS and colophon are registered trademarks of
Simon & Schuster, Inc.

For information about special discounts for bulk purchases,
please contact Simon & Schuster Special Sales at 1-866-506-1949
or business@simonandschuster.com.

The Simon & Schuster Speakers Bureau can bring authors
to your live event. For more information or to book an event
contact the Simon & Schuster Speakers Bureau at 1-866-248-3049
or visit our website at www.simonspeakers.com.

Designed by Jaime Putorti

Manufactured in the United States of America

10 9 8 7 6 5 4 3 2 1

Library of Congress Cataloging-in-Publication Data is available.

ISBN 978-1-4767-0762-4
ISBN 978-1-4767-0763-1 (paperback)
ISBN 978-1-4767-0764-8 (ebook)

DEDICATION

I dedicate this book to the two people who have had the most impact on my life since my divorce: Michael Broussard and Leslie Ann Bruce Amin.

Michael Brousssard, my amazing book "gaygent," my future husband, and my third child. Since meeting you, my life has changed—I now have family in Southern California. Most importantly, thank you for not allowing me to fire you after you left me drunk and lost at a gay bar in Venice when we had barely just met. You truly are "the gift that keeps on giving."

Leslie Ann Bruce Amin, my amazing coauthor of this book, one of the most talented writers that I know, and one of my dearest friends in the world. You are smarter, funnier, and more photogenic than me, and at times brattier than me. I would not be where I am today with out your love, advice, and direction! Thank you for not allowing me to put half-naked pictures of myself on the internet. I love you.

CONTENTS

Are you a vagina owner or a gay? Then you'll want to read this book. Has your partner ever tried to convince you that you were just "born" with HPV? Then you'll definitely want to read this book. Have you woken up one morning in a three-bedroom rental in Encino, only to find your husband is now married to a washed-up country-music singer and you're in the middle of a reality-television meth controversy? You're going to want to pour yourself an extra large glass of sauvignon blanc . . . because you're me.

As a forty-year-old divorcée and a single mom, I am the first to admit that I don't have all the answers. Okay, that's a lie. I actually have answers for everything; I'm just fairly certain they're all wrong. Over the last four years, I've watched my world explode right in front of me, and for the first time ever, my path is completely up to me. No parents, agents, or husbands to tell me where to go, how to act, or what to do next. Sure, it was scary as hell, and sometimes even now I wake up and wonder what happened to my picture-perfect life. But I'd rather struggle with my uncertainty and fear than continue to live a lie. It took me a while to figure that out, because the lie can be comfortable and easy. But I had to ask myself, What kind of life is that?

When I got divorced, I realized I had completely lost my sense of self. I had always identified myself as any number of nouns: daughter, sister, girlfriend, model, friend, wife, mother, occasional amateur pharmacist— you get the point. I spent most of my life happy just squeezing into someone else's idea of the roles I should play. And finally, after four decades of living, two children, and one costly divorce, I am thrilled to be meeting Brandi. And can I be honest? It took me a long time to get to her, but I think she's just amazing.

My journey has not been smooth or without embarrassing hiccups—and by *hiccups*, I mean huge mistakes— but better me than you, right? Hopefully, you can learn from some of my blunders. . . .

I spent my entire life doing what either fell directly into my lap or what other people told me I should do (although I didn't always listen), so you can't fault me for going crazy when given my first glimpse of freedom. Most women make their mistakes during their college years. Well, I didn't go to college. I went to Europe. And while girl-on-girl experimentation and drugs were prevalent, it wasn't quite the same. I had an agent watching me like a total hawk during every waking moment, and I had the pressure of the nineties fashion world on my shoulders. I know it sounds like champagne problems, but when you've had a notoriously beastly supermodel push you off the runway during Paris Fashion Week or helped a "friend" cover her heroin track marks for a runway show, then come talk to me about how high-pressure college is.

Silly mistakes can be fun and adventurous—it's also where my self-discovery happened. However, waking up in the VIP room of a Vegas strip club only to discover that I'd married my former best friend's ex-husband—and tweeted it out to roughly eighty thousand people—is a story I'd sooner forget. I'd also like to forget the one about my husband having an affair with a country-music singer—along with just about every cocktail waitress in LA—but we can't pick all of our battles; sometimes they choose us.

While I don't consider myself a "celebrity," I hope my story will allow you to peek behind the curtain of a true Hollywood breakup. It's so salacious, it might as well be a Lifetime movie. Oh, wait . . .

For the first time ever, I will reveal the dark underbelly of a celebrity breakup—including staged photo ops with paparazzi, tawdry weekly-magazine contracts, and even how social media can be your own worst enemy. So let me offer you my first piece of advice: if you don't already have a prescription for a good antidepressant, go see a doctor. (I recommend Lexapro; they're now making a more cost-effective generic form! Who said health care was failing?)

But this isn't just a breakup book, ladies and gays. As a middle-aged divorcée who is trying to #KeepItSexy, I'm offering this single's guide to getting your life back together for anyone who is in need of a well-deserved pick-me-up and perhaps a little direction. I know what you're thinking: What does this woman know about my struggles? Sure, I'm a former-model-turned-reality-personality living in Beverly Hills. I'm sure most of you are thinking, *Boo-fucking-hoo.* But I didn't always have what I have now. I started out in the ghetto of South Sacramento, getting beat up daily by a neighborhood thug. Yes, I was previously married to a gorgeous Cuban actor, but he almost ruined my life. Yes, I misidentified historical icon and British politician Winston Churchill as an American civil rights activist on national television. And, yes, I'm known for my tiny bathing suits and my lack of a filter. But I'm also a single mom who shamefully had to go to her youngest son's preschool Halloween parade in the outfit I wore on a date the night prior, because I somehow found myself staying over at the Beverly Hills jail, slapped with a well-deserved DUI. And three months after I left my husband over his inability to stop cheating, I sat alone on Christmas Eve looking at Twitter photos of my entire family having a beautiful holiday dinner—without me. Instead, in the center, sat the woman he wouldn't let go. Even my mother-in-law, the light of my life whom I nursed through cancer, was there. I sincerely hope this never happens to you.

My mother taught me three simple truths in this world that everyone should recognize: everybody has been dumped; everybody has a bad day; and everybody hates anal (unless you're gay . . . even then it's a maybe). These are truths, people.

I'm a firm believer that however you come into this

world is how you live your life. I was born on November 16, 1972, feet-first with the umbilical cord wrapped around my neck three times. Despite my dramatic entrance and a few firm smacks from the doctor, I refused to cry. (Let's be honest, I've always enjoyed a good spanking.) Growing up the second of three kids, I had a relatively typical childhood. My father was the local marijuana distributor, my mother regularly failed to wear undergarments, and our gay teenage neighbor lived on our couch. I routinely got into fistfights with our neighborhood bullies, I tweezed my eyebrows within a centimeter of their life trying to mimic the glossy fashion magazines I was obsessed with, and my first kiss was with my cousin "Biffer." Like I said, totally normal. Hindsight being twenty-twenty, it also prepared me perfectly for the world of reality television.

After high school, I spent a year partying in San Francisco, enjoying my fair share of mind-altering drugs, while weaning myself off my Almay shimmery-pink and midnight-blue eyeshade kit (my agent made me get rid of it). Somehow, I stumbled upon a successful modeling career that took me to Paris and Milan at nineteen years old and introduced me to a world of Brazilian bikinis, private jets, and uncircumcised penises. I had never even been on a plane before (and purposefully missed my first flight, out of fear). When I met Eddie at twenty-three years old, he asked me to stop traveling, thereby crippling my career, but I was happy to oblige. I would have done anything for that man. And at twenty-eight, I found myself the Hollywood trophy wife to a little-known, but relatively successful, made-for-TV-movie actor. But what he lacked in public notoriety, he more than made up for with local "star"-fuckers. After eight years of our marriage and his high-profile affair with a country-music singer, I discovered my husband landed more pussy than a Backstreet Boy—back when people actually fucked Backstreet Boys.

It doesn't matter who you are, what you do, or where you live, everybody struggles from time to time. It's not the struggles that define you; it's how you overcome them. Among the many lessons I've learned, here are a few of my favorites:

+ If your husband requires more than one "guys' night" a week, he's either fucking a twenty-year-old cocktail waitress . . . or gay.

+ You don't need a job to go on a $20,000 shopping spree at Neiman Marcus; you just need an

ex-husband, his American Express card, and a
chip on your shoulder.

✦ It's okay to talk about your breast implants; it's
not okay to talk about vaginal rejuvenation.
Even if you get vaginal rejuvenation. Shh!

✦ Do not be ashamed of taking antidepressants;
basically everybody does. Be ashamed if you're
not talking about it.

✦ Your friends will always be your friends . . . as
long as your husband doesn't marry someone
with more money, paparazzi on speed dial, and
a mansion in Nashville.

So get your Kindle, e-reader, iPad, or even good old-
fashioned printed book ready and hunker down with your
favorite blanket, because this girl's guide—complete with
hate sex, plastic surgery, and lesbian make-outs—makes
Fifty Shades of Grey's "red room" seem like a nursery
rhyme.

CHAPTER ONE

If He Walks like a Duck and Talks like a Duck . . . Then He's a Pig

People always say, "Don't panic."

Really? Who are these people? I discovered that my husband of eight years was banging every short skirt—and wide back—in Hollywood after seeing it on the cover of a celebrity-gossip magazine, but I'm supposed to stay calm? I'm supposed to eat shit with a fork and a knife and say thank you when I'm done swallowing this crap?

Fuck off. I'm here to tell you that if your husband, wife, boyfriend, or girlfriend is cheating, life, as you know it, is over. It's the God's honest truth, and anyone who tells you otherwise is either completely blowing smoke up your ass, a lawyer, or my ex-husband.

It's actually quite the contrary. It's time to freak the fuck out, and that's not just acceptable, it's obligatory. The rug has just been pulled out from beneath your feet, and everything you thought you knew with absolute certainty has vanished. Absolute hysteria is just the beginning—you're about to embark on an entire roller coaster of crazy-ass emotions. So I, Brandi Glanville, am here to bestow this simple but valuable piece of information on you: if you discover your partner is cheating, drink like it's your last party, blame everyone else for your problems, let "binging" be your new favorite hobby, and, by all means, FUCKING PANIC.

It was a cold, sunny morning the day my world fell apart.

Sure. There were signs. Like, what man has baby wipes in the center console of his Porsche? Please, like he ever changed a diaper. It's not a science, but I'm pretty certain my husband was getting more than his fair share of roadside assistance.

But, as the saying goes, ignorance is bliss: I had a beautiful, six-bedroom home in Calabasas, a full-time nanny, a brand-new Range Rover, an $11,500 boob job, two wonderful little boys, and a gorgeous Cuban husband. And I was the perfect little Hollywood housewife. Yes, the writing was on the wall that my husband was far from perfect, and, yes, every so often my curiosity would rear its head, but I chose to ignore it because life was good—plus, even if I believed it, I couldn't prove a damn thing—in fact, it was great. So when reports of my husband's infidelities became national news one fateful March morning, I was the lucky recipient of the world's biggest gut punch. (Both Sandra Bullock and Elin Nordegren would soon follow my lead—let's just say Eddie's lucky his golf clubs weren't handy.)

It was just your typical Wednesday. Like clockwork, a sleepy-eyed Mason wandered into our bedroom just before five in the morning. Who needs an alarm clock when you have a six-year-old? And just as I did every morning, I gently tugged him into bed and placed him between Eddie and me. With my finger, I would softly trace letters across his tiny shoulders until his eyelids fluttered and he drifted back to sleep. Eddie would, without opening his eyes, smile and toss his strong, muscular arm over us both and pull us to his chest. Wrapped up in each other's arms, my little family and I would fall away for a few more hours of precious sleep. Oftentimes, I would even lie awake, taking it all in and appreciating how perfect life could be. Not until we heard Jakey's cries would Mason finally say, "Mom, go get your robe." I would crawl out of bed and head down the hallway to release Jake from his kiddie corral with Mason trailing behind me.

The sound of Jake's shrieks would echo through the house until I would finally swing open the door and see my two-year-old sitting behind his baby gate with crocodile tears and a smile from ear to ear. "Faker," I thought, but still I picked him up and hugged him hard until I could feel his little body relax. I couldn't resist that face—or those gorgeous dimples. Well advanced for his two short years, Jake Austin Cibrian not only managed to crawl out of his crib nightly, but he'd also figured out how to open the door to his bedroom. Did I mention that he was still in diapers? This kid would be the death of me.

So being the paranoid and nurturing mama bear,

I had nightmares of my precious baby waddling about in the middle of the night and tumbling down the grand marble stairway or climbing up the banister and falling to his certain death onto the foyer floor below. I know I was being totally irrational, but I decided to put a lock on the outside of his door, because if he was clever enough to climb out of a crib, the baby gate was going to be zero challenge for him. I was aware that this was in strict violation of a number of fire-department building codes, but I didn't care. Seriously though, it isn't as drastic as it sounds, but you try going to Mommy and Me class with a bunch of uptight professional Beverly Hills mothers. Ultimately, if it gave me the peace of mind that he was safe so I could sleep for six uninterrupted hours, then I was willing to do just about anything.

Isn't that the goal with all parenting? Don't kill the kids? Shit, isn't that the goal with every relationship— not killing one another?

When I finally managed to get both of the boys dressed, the three of us headed to the kitchen for our typical morning routine: a breakfast consisting of hard-boiled eggs, Honey Bunches of Oats cereal, and Gatorade, followed by the Round Meadow community car pool and a laundry list of errands to run before the trip to Parrot Cay Eddie and I were planning that weekend. My best friend was getting married to the man of her dreams—who just so happened to be Hollywood's biggest movie star, Bruce Willis—and it was the first time in months that Eddie and I were escaping for a grown-ups vacation. No babies and no BlackBerrys; just my handsome husband and me.

Let's be clear, Eddie and I had an extremely healthy sex life (so where he got all that extra energy, I'll never be sure), but every so often we would run away together so we could make love in the middle of the afternoon as loud as we wanted, for as long as we wanted. And he would kiss me the way he did when we had nothing but time. That, coupled with an occasional lesbian make-out, was the recipe for our seemingly successful marriage. I know what you're thinking: how was it okay for *me* to hook up with other women, but not my husband? Welcome to La La Land, ladies and gays. If you don't keep your man satisfied, there is some other hussy who will. I thought keeping things spicy in the bedroom was the only surefire way to keep my man from straying. #LessonLearned. I'm not talking about any below-the-belt action, just some harmless grab-assing and sexy making out. I can definitely appreciate a pretty girl, so on occasion I would hook up with girlfriends, so that my husband could watch. (Sometimes the girl had a boyfriend or husband, too, who also seemed to enjoy the show.) It was harmless and Eddie seemed to appreciate it, because without fail, it would lead to some pretty hot sex afterward. Like I said, I was just an average Hollywood housewife doing whatever I could to keep my husband happy.

After breakfast and midway through an episode of *Mickey Mouse Clubhouse*, I popped a toothbrush in each boy's mouth and began packing Mason's lunch. Right on cue, Eddie dropped into the kitchen to give the boys and me our morning-ritual "love bug" kiss (where all of our lips met) before heading off for the gym—already fully showered. (Again, you would think a little alarm would go off, but nothing.) Little did I know that our simple, boring morning encounter would be the last time I would ever see the man I married, my Eddie. He gave me a tap on my booty—his favorite part of my body, which he often referred to as my "upside-down heart"— and flashed me one of his toothy, crooked smiles, complete with those dimples that I loved so much. (Flash forward: Eddie ended up getting Invisalign to straighten his teeth from crooked to perfectly perfect. Now if only he could do the same to his crooked-ass lies.)

Then he disappeared, as he always did, into the garage. I went about my morning in blissful ignorance. After getting my babies dressed, fed, and loaded into the car (no easy task since the nanny was nowhere to be found, but, then again, the house was ten thousand square feet), I finally arrived at the seventh circle of hell: the Round Meadow car-pool drop-off line. In what universe is it normal to wait forty minutes to drop your kids off at school? Welcome to the Valley, ladies and gentlemen, the land of horses and divorces. No wonder everyone who lives here pops more pills than a *Celebrity Rehab* cast member. Once I finally navigated the drop-off lane, I sent Mason and my carful of grade-schoolers (minus Jake) off to their classes. "Finally," I thought, as I headed back toward home, a three-minute drive if you're not waiting in a car-pool line. I needed to get Jakey home to our nanny, who I assumed was awake by now. I just had to find her, before heading to meet my private Pilates trainer of the last six years. (Ladies and gays, if you are thirty-five or older and are looking to change your body, Pilates is the only option. Trust me. I'm forty years old today and I'm feeling as confident as ever.) Just as I hit my ostentatious neighborhood gates, I heard my phone buzz. It was a text message from a "friend"—aka a total fucking hater—and the second wife of one of Eddie's sleazy-ass friends.

This woman—an incredibly bored woman who broke up her current husband's previous marriage and resented that I was still close friends with his first wife— was all too eager to alert me to a story on *PerezHilton*. She texted me that the blog had posted the accusation that my husband was having an affair. Most people would freak the fuck out, right? That's the only normal, natural response. And that's my advice. But as you will quickly learn, my darlings, do as I say, not as I do.

When I read the text again, my immediate reaction was to burst into uncontrollable nervous laughter. This had to be a joke, right? Even if there was any truth to it, why would *PerezHilton* ever care enough to publish a story about my husband? This "friend" seriously expected me to believe that someone put Eddie Cibrian on one of the most popular celebrity websites? Please. He was just a little-known made-for-television-movie actor. He had managed a pretty consistent soap opera career, but my husband was far from a household name, and in no world (other than *Playgirl*, or perhaps *Out*) would he be worthy of any magazine cover. Don't get me wrong, I was always proud of him. I considered Eddie one of the most handsome men alive and appreciated the life his career provided for us, but when it came to his acting, I was under no delusions. Eddie was pretty. Actually, he was fucking gorgeous (and he knew it), but the man is not the most talented actor. I always thought Eddie's calling should have been professional sports (I mean, he did have more affairs than an NBA player), but he wanted to be an actor. Our boys were blessed with his athletic build, but their coordination . . . question mark. Maybe that wouldn't have been the case if Eddie had actually been around the first few years of their lives, but the boys have come around and are now great little athletes.

Eddie started acting because he was hot as hell and it came easy for him (much like the abundance of pussy he surrounded himself with). Despite earning an impressive football scholarship to UCLA (he played strong safety), he decided to quit midway through his junior year to join the cast of the TV soap *The Young and the Restless*. He looked fantastic on camera, but he was never winning any Academy Awards.

I grew up in the modeling world. At seventeen years old, I was plucked out of a mall in Sacramento, California. I was told to change my hair color, forced to abandon my midnight-blue eyeliner, and was strictly forbidden to taking tweezers to my eyebrows. I was told I was a body girl and didn't have the kind of face for beauty work. I was tormented by some of the most well-known agents and supermodels in the business, so the idea of putting on kid gloves to nurse Eddie's acting blues was never something I considered. Every so often, I relented and spent a few minutes stroking my husband's ego. Little did I know that my husband was already getting a fair amount of stroking elsewhere.

Eddie Cibrian was a working television actor with a gorgeous smile that paid our bills and afforded our life. That was all I cared about: Eddie and our children. I didn't need to be married to Brad Pitt—I just wanted Eddie. He was, but hopefully won't always be, the love of my life. And love can be blinding. However, when you choose to remove your love goggles, a good prescription pill might be in order.

The text about the *PerezHilton* post wasn't the first time rumors had swirled among our group of friends about Eddie's wandering eye. Every so often, I would pick up on little whispers about my husband's extra-curricular activities, and when I'd confront him, he'd say, "You're crazy!" He never hesitated to calm my insecurities and convince me how totally insane it was for me to question his total devotion to our family and me. I fell for it every time: hook, line, and sinker. The lies that he could tell were astounding. I mean, could you ever convince your significant other that you caught HPV simply by sharing a lollipop with a colleague? Or then try to argue that you had actually been born with it, and it just didn't show up for thirty-five years?

Yes, this raises more questions than answers. For example, what grown man sucks on a lollipop? (Clearly, he was sucking on a whole lot of things.) That's a little weird. And why, if making the decision to be a grown man sucking on a lollipop, would you actually share it with another person besides your wife or children?

In the end, I guess he *did* actually end up sharing it with me.

These are all questions I should have demanded the answers to, before undergoing three surgeries to remove cancerous cells caused by the strand of HPV that was discovered after we had already been married for years. My doctor said it was almost certain I got it from my husband. (Oh, just so you know, you can only catch HPV by having sex with someone else who has the disease or if it was one of the rare cases when it's passed on during childbirth. And never from a lollipop.) So even if our marriage didn't last, I will always have a certain "something" to remember him by. Thanks, Eddie. Couldn't he have contracted something curable, like the clap?

I would confide my concerns to friends, who would say, "B, he adores you. You're crazy." I had a perfect life, so I chalked up the rumors to jealousy and decided all of my concerns were crazy. Seriously, when would he even have the time? We were rarely without one another while he wasn't "working," and he was equally curious as to my whereabouts. I always figured that occasional jealously kept both of us on our toes and kept our relationship spicy. What husband or wife doesn't want to think that his or her partner is desirable to other people? It's all part of the game, because "the challenge" is key for just about any relationship—especially in LA. They don't call it a *trophy* spouse for nothing.

I was so certain that this text message was a joke made in the most miserable of tastes that when Eddie called moments later, I was cool and breezy when I answered the phone. "Hey, babe," I purred.

It didn't take long after that for my entire life to begin unraveling—and I could do absolutely nothing to hold it all together. "There's a story in *Us Weekly*," he said, failing to mention that it was on the fucking cover.

"Oh," I said, playing dumb.

He immediately spiraled into what turned out to be a whirlwind of lies. He rattled off some story about him and LeAnn Rimes having dinner in Laguna Beach, as an act of charity to help out a friend in a struggling marriage.

LeAnn. It all started to make sense now. It wasn't my husband who was the big draw to the glossy celebrity-tabloid world, but rather a certain country-music singer who was my husband's recent made-for-TV costar. Maybe it was his too-forceful denial or maybe it was that

I never really trusted him, but in that moment I knew my life was about to change. But just how drastically, I could never have known.

Truth be told, I had already suspected for months. I recalled when she sat across the dining-room table from me, telling me how hilarious Eddie was on set. Ladies and gentlemen, Eddie Cibrian is many, many, many things—the former member of a failed Canadian pop trio, perhaps?—but humorous is not one of them. LeAnn's then husband, Dean Sheremet, and I shared more than one look across the table. He knew, too. We were both visiting our spouses while they were on the Calgary set of *Northern Lights*—Dean actually stayed on location during the majority of filming. Not until I insisted upon meeting his little Nashville costar did Eddie set up a double date at a nearby sushi restaurant. And this woman, whom I had just met, spent more time flirting with my husband than acknowledging her own. And Dean, bless his heart, ate his sushi, laughed at all the right moments, and pretended that he didn't see exactly what was in front of him. As the evening progressed, every time LeAnn made some sort of inappropriate advance toward my husband—a whisper, a giggle, or a reach across the ever-shrinking table—Eddie squeezed my hand a little tighter. And as if on cue, Eddie would lean over the table, every so often, to offer me a nervous, overly tongue-y kiss to gauge my current state of mind. I decided that it wasn't my husband's doing; she was just a child star who had married young and was unhappy with her own marriage. It couldn't be anything else. It couldn't be anything else, because it appeared to me that she was both very married and not at all Eddie's type. I can definitely appreciate a beautiful woman (I'm a total waist-up lesbian), but I didn't find her at all attractive. When later that same night LeAnn awkwardly pulled my husband (not hers!) onstage for an awful karaoke rendition of Sonny and Cher's "I Got You Babe," I just about lost it. (Side note: that was the song they danced to at their wedding three years later. Sweet, right? And not at all creepy or insanely inappropriate?)

Was she serious? I felt that I was in the twilight zone. I sat there waiting for Ashton Kutcher to jump out from behind the bar, because I was certain I was on *Punk'd*. Being the devoted housewife and trusting partner, I wasn't going to say anything to them, but I knew that kind of tenacity didn't come from nowhere. I looked at

Eddie's smiling face on that stupid, low-rent stage and leaned over to Dean and said, "You know they're fucking, right?"

Dean didn't say anything—which said just about everything I needed to know. He knew it, too, but, like me, didn't have any evidence besides that gut feeling, and he chose to ignore it for now. I went back to sipping my wine and kept quiet. On the outside, I appeared calm and casual; on the inside, I was going fucking insane, cursing the day I convinced Eddie to do this film and meet this horrible woman. That was, until the final fucking straw.

LeAnn had "accidentally" smeared some cake frosting on her top (she was still a bigger girl and completely flat-chested at the time) and asked my husband, not realizing that I was standing behind the both of them, if he wanted to lick it off her. This woman asked my husband if he wanted to eat the frosting mess she'd dropped on her nonexistent chest? Are you fucking kidding me? He hadn't realized I was there either, and he laughed with hungry eyes at the suggestion.

I immediately stepped in between the two lovebirds, well aware that I was positioning my ass in my husband's crotch (you know the drill), and coyly asked the pair,

"What the fuck do you two have going on? Do you two have something you'd like to tell me?"

LeAnn laughed through her oversized dentures before purring, "Oh, honey, you're just being silly."

People can call me a lot of things, but I know what I saw, and this married chick was not about to convince me otherwise. I went back to the table, grabbed my purse, and got the hell out of there. I don't know if my husband even came home that night. (But I can't imagine he went home with LeAnn and Dean. I assume that they had a few things to talk about, too). Eddie and I had adjoining rooms, so I locked the door and slept with Mason (my then five-year-old and the real love of my life). We woke up early the next morning and jumped in a cab to the airport. I flew home convinced that my husband was having an affair with this woman.

Ironically, I was the one who actually convinced Eddie to do this Lifetime movie. He was a lucky working TV "actor" coming off guest spots on a few television shows (*Ugly Betty*, *The Starter Wife*, *Samantha Who?*—so strange that they all were canceled shortly after he joined); he thought he was "too big" to do a made-for-TV movie. But I knew we needed the money, because his mother—who managed all of our finances—told me as much. I mean, clearly I wasn't given any access to our bills, because Shady McShaderson had almost all of our bills sent to his parents' house. So, I encouraged him to take the role and the paycheck. Plus, being a jealous wife, I always was concerned with who his costar would be. But LeAnn Rimes? I thought it couldn't get much safer. I was much more at peace when my husband, and the father of my children, was playing opposite a married woman. Oh, boy . . . was I wrong. Child stars are just about the worst. Throughout their careers, no one ever tells them no; they just assume that they can take anything they want without any repercussions.

When Eddie finally got ahold of me the next day after I had retuned to Los Angeles, he convinced me that I was just being paranoid. I even asked him about the frosting incident, and he told me, "You see and hear things that don't actually happen." I wanted to believe him so desperately that I let him convince me that I just made it up in my head. Apparently Dean was delusional, as well. I was a sweep-it-under-the-rug kind of girl—had been my whole married life. It's shocking how oblivious you can allow yourself to be. And it's even more shocking how much the truth can still hurt, despite knowing it in the back of your head all along. My marriage was a heartbreaking sham, and I was completely blindsided, because I chose to accept the fantasy and to keep wearing those love goggles—*chose* being the operative word. I chose to believe/fantasize that through our eight-year marriage that my husband was faithful. Now, it literally makes me laugh out loud.

That fateful Wednesday when the story broke, my phone conversation with Eddie ended in a hot blur. I'm not entirely sure how I ended up on the floor of my closet sobbing, but I can only assume it was an instinctual attraction to the only thing that could ever bring me peace: my shoes. A teary-eyed Eddie found me lying there minutes later, and without saying so much as a word, he started kissing me all over. He pulled off my workout pants and we started having sex right there in front of Manolo, Christian, and Jimmy. Yet another huge red flag that our relationship was six different kinds of fucked-up. He swore up and down my body that it wasn't true; that it was just a string of disconnected photos that didn't tell the actual story; that he didn't tell me he was meeting her because he knew I would be mad and that it was completely innocent. In that moment, it was easier to believe him, because I just couldn't stand the thought of being without him. We had a trip to go on, and I had some super-tiny bikinis to run around in. Okay, I decided to go with the fantasy and believe he wasn't actually cheating on me. Like always, it must have been all in my head.

If only I could have been prepared for how wrong I was.

We spent the weekend in the Caribbean, just as I had planned: drinking all day on the beach and making love on crisp white sheets. We didn't talk about what would happen when we returned home, because we were caught up in the weekend. It was a perfect getaway, and it felt like just what the doctor ordered. Plus, I was trying to be strong for my best friend. I didn't want to make this weekend about anything other than her beautiful wedding. Eddie never mentioned the affair; my best friend married her soul mate; Winston Churchill remained a civil rights activist; and everything was right with the world. But in the back of my mind, I knew this was our last hurrah—our D-list Jen-and-Brad beach moment. We were saying good-bye to our lives as we knew them. The sex was unbelievable, because I think we were unsure if we would ever make love again. I was certain we would have sex again, but truly make love? I didn't think so. Eddie and I landed in Miami after our trip to Parrot Cay and returned to reality, and, boy, did reality bite.

I finally turned my phone back on and realized that not only did I have an obscene number of text messages, but my voice-mail box was full, too. Sure, I had a ton of family and friends, but this was ridiculous. When Eddie turned on his phone and started scrolling through his messages, it looked as if he had seen a ghost. I knew right then that I wasn't actually crazy. Something else had happened.

The many, many messages had a common theme: there was video. *Us Weekly* had posted surveillance footage from the restaurant where Eddie and LeAnn had dinner. The video even captured intimate moments of my husband with this other woman: kissing one another, licking and sucking on one another's fingers. If that wasn't enough, it was available for the world to see. Couldn't it at least have been Cindy Crawford? If that were the case, I might have asked to join the party. But, no, it was a has-been country-music singer.

Eddie had absolutely nothing to say. What could he say at that point? He just looked at me with pain in his eyes. I don't think Eddie regrets much in his life, but in that moment, I knew he regretted the pain he was causing me. But more important, he regretted getting caught—and it couldn't get much more red-handed than this. Thank God I never actually walked in on him with another woman; I would have killed them both. Eddie's eyes were clearly no longer on the prize. Or, maybe, I just wasn't the prize anymore.

So there we were. Eddie was catching a flight to DC to shoot a television pilot, and I was heading back to Los Angeles to see our boys. We were parting ways there in the middle of an airport. It remains one of the most defining moments of my life: sitting in a crappy, plastic airport chair watching my husband, the love of my life, walk away from me—and from us. Doesn't that moment at least deserve a La-Z-Boy? A gliding rocking chair perhaps? Or how about a hospital bed with a morphine drip? In any event, I quickly found the nearest bar stool. It wasn't going to be an easy journey, and there would be plenty of setbacks, but I wasn't going to be the victim. It was time for me to put my big-girl panties on and reclaim my life. When life hands you lemons, grab the nearest bottle of vodka and make yourself a cocktail.

The moral of the story couldn't be clearer: you already know if your partner is fucking around behind your back, you just need to decide if you're done being a doormat. You need to wake up one morning and decide that those rose-colored glasses are so last fucking season.

Always remember that you are a beautiful, strong woman or gay, and that plenty of wonderful men (and, perhaps, women) want to bend you over a kitchen table . . . or couch. I'm an equal-opportunity furniture molester.

Once you've decided to regain control of your life, the next step is to catch him in the act. Or, hypothetically, tape a phone conversation between the two of you in which he admits to fucking you on the staircase of your formerly shared home just a few days earlier, despite already living with his mistress; in which he admits that she is unattractive, that he doesn't actually love her and would never marry her; and then asks you to come meet him at the McDonald's he is at with the kids, because he wants you to take him back. After it's all recorded, send her ass the tape . . . hypothetically.

If at all possible, don't get married in California. That "no-fault state" business can be a real shit show, because despite the insane levels of douchebaggery, your alimony check won't go up, and all you have to lose is the only thing you have left: your dignity.

If you still have questions about your partner's fidelity, here are my top five signs that he is cheating:

1. He has two cell phones and no job.

2. He showers *before* going to the gym.

3. Your partner all of sudden requires a lot more "me" time. Especially if your partner is Eddie Cibrian—that man had more "me" time than most single guys.

4. Local business meetings never require an overnight stay. Never.

5. His credit card bills and cell phone bills go to his parents' house.

If you are able to check off any of these, it's time to reevaluate your relationship. If you can check off three or more, you're fucked. Number five may not actually be a

barometer of his cheating, but it's douchey either way—
especially at thirty-five.

And while this is by no means a definitive list, I'd like
to think it's a pretty good temperature read. But it's not
brain science or rocket surgery. If the ground is wet and
the sky is gray, it's probably raining (or you woke up in
a VIP room full of strippers at the Spearmint Rhino in
Vegas).

brandi's **babble**

Before you judge the girl with the broken ankle, walk a
mile in her stiletto.

CHAPTER TWO

It's a Breakup, Not Cancer

The most surprising thing about breaking up is that you already know how to do it. Everything you need to know, you learned in kindergarten.

- Yours should always be better than his (especially when it comes to lawyers).

- Sharing sucks.

- A nice glass of grape juice can cure just about anything.

- Always wait to be called on before speaking (in both mediations and the courtroom).

✦ And finally, always remember that the other
person started it.

For obvious reasons, a breakup is much easier if
you're (a) not married and (b) don't have kids. But the
division of assets (and friends!) is always challenging.

If you are married and making the command decision to get a divorce, the first thing you do is lawyer
up. It's probably the hardest move to make, because
you're actually admitting to yourself that you're getting
divorced. No more what-if scenarios or "maybe I'll wake
up from this nightmare" pipe dreams. It's about to happen, and it's harder and longer than childbirth—without
an epidural. Eddie handled everything in our relationship, so I had no idea where to start. Computers were
(and still sort of are) foreign objects to me, and I was
just starting to learn how to use one, but the concept of
"googling" divorce attorneys was not an option. Instead,
I went with word of mouth. I got a laundry list of sug-
gestions of amazing lawyers with stellar reputations, but
when it finally came to making the calls, I had a rude
awakening. I was told—one after the other—that representing me would be a conflict of interest. How could it

be that every good lawyer in Los Angeles was representing my husband? It took me a bit to learn this valuable divorce lesson (so listen close): whichever party contacts a lawyer first, that attorney, by law, cannot represent the other party. I quickly figured out that my soon-to-be ex-husband—most likely at the suggestion of his fancy lawyer—had had the foresight to call every decent lawyer in the area for a meeting before I did. It was his way of legally crippling me. Not only was this going to be ugly, but I was also going to get fucked—and not in the good way.

One of my best girlfriends had just gone through a divorce and suggested her lawyer. Nothing fancy, but she was apparently totally fair and kept her legal fees to a minimum. Ironically, this is the same best friend who now vacations with LeAnn and Eddie. #JustSayin. I met with this lawyer and hired her on the spot. She was a bit of a ballbuster, and I figured that would come in handy if Eddie decided to play hardball. She also told me I wouldn't have to fork over a dime up front, because her entire fee would come out of the settlement. I felt good about my decision. I was being rational, reasonable, and not working from a place of emotions.

And, let's be honest, I didn't have two nickels to rub together.

My ex-husband, on the other hand, went out and hired the most high-profile celebrity-divorce attorney in Los Angeles, Neal Hersh—with Eddie not realizing that he wasn't actually a high-profile celebrity himself . . . and neither was his girlfriend, for that matter. He went out and hired a total bulldog to nail my ass to a wall. I never stood a chance.

In spite of everything, that's the one thing I never understood. After thirteen years and two children, this man was intent on ruining me. And why? Because I discovered that he fucked half of Hollywood? Because I wasn't going to be a doormat anymore and finally stood up for myself in the media? How is that my fault? But that was just another piece in this painful puzzle. I had no idea who he was anymore, and I was beginning to realize I never did.

Like I said, Eddie handled everything having to do with bills, loans, insurance, etc. I handled the kids. I think up until that point, Eddie had never spent one night alone with the boys. But raising his children,

I discovered, offered me zero insurance when it came to divorce. In all of our years of marriage, I did not have my name on a single document—not for any of the homes we purchased, not one of the cars or motorcycles. Every credit card, every power bill, every medical statement was in my husband's name. Even the vintage Bronco my father had given us to refurbish was in Eddie's name. In thirteen years, I had built precisely zero credit. I had zero savings. And now, I was about to become a single mom.

Someone told me that I should wait for him to file first, so that he would incur the cost. That was the stupidest advice ever. When it comes to divorce, the $2,000 charge that the city charges you to process the divorce isn't even a blip on the radar. After nearly two years of back-and-forth, Eddie's and my divorce cost north of $250,000. I know that doesn't seem like a costly divorce to certain people in LA, but to us, it was beyond substantial. We had been living beyond our means for years—and despite the occasional hints from his mother ("Brandi, you guys are spending too much money," she would say), I was pretty much in the dark about it. I figured she wanted us to be frugal since the downturn in the economy, but Eddie never stopped buying expensive toys or planning luxurious vacations. Toward the end of our marriage, he even paid cash for a new Harley-Davidson. I went with him to the bank and saw him pull out the wad of cash. So I didn't worry too much about it. That wasn't my job in the relationship. I had a hot dinner served on time every night, and I looked great on his arm. That was my role.

Not until we started the divorce did I realize how truly broke we were. Yet another opportunity for Eddie to smack me in the face with something I was so unprepared for.

I grew up in a modest home with a modest household income. My father was the local pot dealer, and my mom was a hippie who rarely wore a bra. I was the middle child between my older sister, Tricia, and my younger brother, Michael (both of whom still live in Northern California). My mother breast-fed us far too long, and my father worked three jobs, besides the pot dealing, so we rarely saw him. I know it sounds awful—"my father, the drug dealer"—but it truly was a means to an end. He sold pot because it was an extra income that could help to send all three of us to a private Lutheran school outside our neighborhood. We lived in a terrible neighborhood, and the public schools around us were dangerous.

Sure, I became used to the fancy house and the nice things, but I was never afraid of living a modest life again, if we needed to. I would have scaled back enormously, had I known how much we were hurting, and tried to pitch in any way I could. It was a marriage, a partnership. We lived in Los Angeles, surrounded by some of the wealthiest people in the world, but Eddie and I were never truly rich. We were ghetto rich—we had the nice cars, the nice house, and the nice jewels, but we probably had a second and a third mortgage. We were living paycheck to paycheck, with little savings.

You can imagine the insane frustration I felt when it cost me a quarter of a million dollars just to divorce a man who was parking his Harley in every available spot in town. In hindsight, I wish I'd had the emotional satisfaction of filing first, so I wouldn't ever have to hear again that it was Eddie who left me. In actuality, I ended things. He would have come back if I let him, but that wasn't an option. I would never be able to look at him the same way again.

The divorce would probably have cost us less than

50 percent of what it did if we had chosen a mediator, but what did Eddie care? He had a sugar mama now. He was angry, and he always had to win.

After the news came out that Eddie and LeAnn were having an affair, gossip reporters bombarded me hoping to score some outrageous quotes (and, boy, did they eventually get some juicy one-liners from me). I have no idea how they figured out my cell phone number, but the calls were coming morning, noon, and night. And they weren't harassing just me, they were going after my friends and family, too. During the early stages of the media chaos, I kept quiet, because Eddie and I were trying to make things work. We signed up for couples therapy before news of his second affair, with the cocktail waitress, made headlines. (Word to the wise: if you need to see a couples therapist, your marriage is probably already over.) He even bought me a stripper pole for our anniversary. (Looking back, I see that was probably a pretty big red flag.) I didn't realize that the entire time we were in therapy and trying to save our marriage, he was still seeing LeAnn.

Once photos surfaced of Eddie and LeAnn on motorcycles in Malibu, I just lost my shit. The same afternoon those pictures were taken, the *In Touch* magazine photos of Eddie and Sheena the cocktail waitress (also known by me as his Tuesday-night slut) were circulating online and brought to my attention. In his defense, he did tell me that he was playing poker every Tuesday night. Silly me, I thought he was playing a card game. I didn't realize that he was actually playing "poke her." I guess it's my fault for not asking him to spell it?

When I saw the Sheena photos, I immediately packed a bag and announced to Eddie that I was moving into the Beverly Hills Hotel. He begged me not to go, but I was determined to make my point and have him watch me walk away. Apparently, as soon as I hit the door, he was off to see LeAnn. I thought I was going to teach him a lesson; instead I learned that I just sent him right into her arms. But I guess he was headed that way, anyway.

No one ever tells you about the nitty-gritty of divorce. For instance, I never imagined my husband and me walking through our shared home of three years with yellow legal pads, picking apart what each of us would be keeping. It was one of the most surreal experiences of my life: each of us flanked by our lawyers, we went from room to room, slowly and meticulously deconstructing the life we had spent years building together. While we agreed on many items, Eddie was going to fight me for some of the big-ticket items, including the twelve-person Tiffany dinnerware set we received as a wedding gift from my parents. Like, for real, dude? You want to split our china? He did. And he got half. So if anyone is interested, I can do a posh dinner party for six on Tiffany china. I lost the crystal glassware, though, so it's BYOC (bring your own cup) at my next dinner party . . . for six.

During further negotiations, I sat across the table from him in one of those big, cold conference rooms. It was so surreal to me, because I was able to see a side of him that I never recognized before. He was a coward. In retrospect, I'm surprised he even had the fucking balls to show up. He's hidden behind lies and half-truths his entire life, so anytime he's faced with brutal honesty, he runs. It's just his nature. And part of me was all too happy to insult him in front of his fancy-pants lawyer.

We fought over the motorcycles, the condo, the boat, and the electronics . . . everything. I even brought in a forensic accountant to dissect his credit-card bills to dig up what he purchased for his mistress with our joint funds. It cost me $12,000 to find out that he bought his Tuesday-night girlfriend some diamond earrings and paid the rent for her Hollywood apartment. The irony? I didn't even get any money for it, and I still had to pay the bill. But I was angry and hurt, so I was up for the fight. It became the ultimate pissing match. I spent double what I ended up getting as the settlement, just because I wanted to fight with him, and I didn't want him to win.

Eddie even fought me for the Bronco my father had given us to refurbish. That's where I nearly lost it. I was planning to give it back to my father. When I told my dad that Eddie was fighting me for it, he called Eddie to tell him that it was a gift meant for me. Eddie might be a total loser, but he just loves to win.

Determining ownership of the Bronco was one of the final sticking points in our divorce. During one of our last meetings, the lawyers suggested that we each write down on a piece of paper how much we were willing to spend to buy the Bronco off the other person. The person with the highest number would pay that to the other party out of the settlement. We both agreed.

I knew Eddie wanted to win and that he would pay a premium to get the car. I would have loved to get it, but I couldn't afford to lose that money out of our settlement. I had no income and decided that I needed to let it go, but Eddie didn't have to know that. So, I decided to try to milk some money out of the bastard. With my pen, I pretended to write a large, long figure on my piece of paper. I noticed Eddie doing the same. We both pushed our papers to the middle of the table, and our lawyers flipped them around. Eddie was willing to pay $65,000. I was willing to pay $1. Eddie pretended that he didn't care that I just screwed him out of $65,000, but I knew it royally pissed him off. What could be sweeter? I got paid a whole lot of money to irritate my ex-husband.

But in the same vein, did I want half of his fancy tools? You bet your ass. Did I try to snake half of his watch collection? Obviously. But Eddie was smart— smarter than he looks, anyway. I remember watching him carry the watch case filled with his extravagant watch collection (including three Rolexes, three Panerais, two Franck Mullers, and a Cartier that I had given him, totaling well over $100,000) out of the house the very day news of his affair had come out, along with many of the expensive electronics. This was the love of my life and our marriage was over, so naturally that sent me into a tailspin. It was clear to me then that this was going to get ugly.

Luckily, I was able to keep my wedding rings: a three-carat, prong-set wedding band and my four-and-a-quarter-carat, princess-cut, center-stone engagement ring. Today it's probably worth upward of $70,000 and could probably have saved me a lot of financial hardship in the beginning had I decided to sell it, but I just couldn't. Instead, I locked the ring away in a safe-deposit box, so that one day my Mason or Jake can have it. People often ask me if I think it would be bad luck for my son and future daughter-in-law to use a ring that was the symbol of my failed marriage. My answer? Fuck off. How could a thirteen-year relationship that brought into this world two of its most beautiful people be considered a failure or bad luck? I don't regret being Eddie's wife, and I don't regret the life we built together. I just regret encouraging him to do that made-for-TV movie.

After the division of the assets came the really fun part, the child- and spousal-support negotiations. This, the lengthiest part of the divorce, lasted over a year. We

BRANDI **GLANVILLE**

couldn't agree on anything, and our lawyers seemed to encourage the fighting (which translated into more billable hours for them). I wanted full custody of my kids, but Eddie was fighting me for half. I know Eddie loves our children, but while we were married, he was never around. He just wasn't a hands-on dad back then. I doubt he even knew how to bathe them or get them ready for bed.

Eventually, after months and months of back-and-forth on who would get what, I backed down—as I always did with him. It just wasn't worth it anymore, and it was draining the life out of me. I was exhausted, depressed, and drinking too much for my own good. I was in a bad place. It simply wasn't healthy to exert this much time and energy on hate and revenge. The continued fighting was consuming me, fucking me up. I concluded that I kept fighting with him to keep him in my life in some capacity. In my head, all of our arguments came from a place of passion. I realized that I was holding on to something that wasn't there anymore. I guess I hadn't been ready to completely let him go. But it was finally time.

Nearly a year and a half after I got that Wednesday-morning call, I was free. Strangely, I don't even remember the exact date, but it was in late September 2010. My lawyer called to tell me the papers were ready to be signed, so I drove to her office and signed them. It was surprisingly anticlimactic. Eight years of marriage became null and void with a single signature, but I didn't cry. I didn't even tell any of my friends or family—not because I was hiding it, but because it didn't even register to me that it was something I ought to share. It was a nonevent in my eyes. My marriage had been over for quite some time. I was in a new relationship, and Eddie was already living with LeAnn and would soon be married again, so I didn't see the point in announcing, "I'm officially divorced, peeps!" Instead, I went on with my day. *My* day. I no longer was the dutiful wife. My life, however messy and dysfunctional, was now mine.

brandi's **babble**

Next time, do yourself a favor and get a prenup.

CHAPTER THREE

The Third Kind of Job

To this point in my life, the only jobs I'd ever had to worry about were boob jobs and blow jobs—anything beyond that was simply not in my wheelhouse.

During my senior year of high school, a modeling agent from San Francisco had approached me while I was wandering around the local mall looking for something fab from Contempo Casuals for the weekend ahead. I know what you're thinking: Aren't these the kind of scams that trick idealistic teenage girls into doing soft-core porn? Yep, but mine was totally legit, I swear. The following week, my boyfriend drove me into San Francisco to meet with Al, an agent at Look Models, to discuss my opportunities. Even as graduation quickly approached, I didn't put much thought into what I would do next. I figured I would move to San Francisco (or "the city," as us Sacramento folk called it), get a high-paying serving job at some hip restaurant that only catered to the coolest of people, and spend the next few years partying. Hey, it seemed plausible at the time.

I never had dreams of going to college, joining a sorority, and earning some degree in psychology, social science, or medicine—that all sounded as about appealing to me as virgin sex.

So when this modeling agent expressed interest in me, I just figured modeling was what I was meant to be doing. We sat in his office on O'Farrell Street near Union Square, the heart of the city's fashion district, where he gave me a punch list of self-improvements to make over the next few months. He told me to come back to see him only if they were all satisfied. I consider it my first-ever job training.

1. Immediately color my hair a less offensive shade of blond.

2. Break up with my longest relationship to date: an eye-shadow set of shimmery pink and light blue.

3. Throw my tweezers in the garbage and don't
   touch my eyebrows until directed.

My then-boyfriend, Joey Monahan, was so thrilled
at the prospect that he could soon be dating a "model"
that he readily offered to pay for the insanely overpriced,
high-end hairstylist the agent recommended, named Ron
Pernell. I not-so-humbly accepted. Joey was even okay
with the furry caterpillars growing above my eyes and
my new, more natural makeup look, although it was far
too boring for my taste.

Even then, I knew I would dump Joey. He was crazy
hot, five years older than me, and totally obsessed with
me. He taught me some valuable lessons that would
come in handy for the rest of my life—basically all my
favorite bedroom tricks. He was exactly what every
seventeen-year-old girl in the nineties wanted: Brandon
Walsh. Perhaps that's too dated for some of you, but
unfortunately, I can't name anyone on a CW show. But
I was on to something bigger. I was going to break out
of the Sacramento bubble and do something extraordi-
nary with my life. After an intense eyebrow shaping and
the successful purging of my eye-shadow kit, my agent

offered me an official modeling contract that would take me overseas immediately. Joey transformed into Mr. Not-So-Supportive when he decided that he didn't want me traveling, after all. Instead, he thought I should stay in Sacramento and attend a local junior college. Was he fucking nuts? I had the chance of a lifetime, but I was just supposed to retreat back home?

I decided it was time to leave his ass, but only after he gave me a ride to the airport. Actually, it took me two attempts to board an airplane to Paris at San Francisco International Airport. On the first attempt, I purposefully missed my flight after discovering that I had an absolutely paralyzing fear of flying—one that still haunts me and requires a prescription pill. At a "friend's" suggestion, I headed to San Francisco's Mission District and bought some pills that would help me pass out. The dealer told me it was the equivalent of taking a Valium. I popped the pill before takeoff and woke up only when the flight attendant started shaking me to see if I wanted food; apparently I had "roofied" myself. Yep, the date-rape drug. After ten hours and a few hallucinations, I woke up on the runway of Charles de Gaulle Airport.

I found myself eight thousand miles away from

everything I had ever known and was now living in a completely foreign city. I didn't speak the language and soon figured out that I can't fucking stand French food. (I wish Mexico had a high-fashion scene; I could eat tacos every night.) It was both terrifying and exhilarating. I was ready for this adventure.

I can appreciate now how this opportunity fell into my lap, but I like to think that God front-loaded my life with blessings, knowing that one day I would have to deal with Eddie.

A driver was waiting for me at the airport, a luxury that was completely lost on me at the time. I seriously figured that everybody must have a driver pick him or her up at the airport—maybe it was built into the price of the ticket? I had no frame of reference. The driver was to take me directly to the agency in Paris. I was hoping that after a ten-hour flight and a drug-induced haze that I would at least have a few minutes to freshen up, but no such luck. When you're seventeen years old, I guess you can never look that bad. Plus, I suppose they figured they would be seeing me during a lot of hazy moments, so they might as well be prepared. They would have been right to think that. #PartyAnimal.

When I arrived at the agency, they told me I would be moving into the "models' apartment," with other models from around the world, all of whom were even more stunning than the pictures in their portfolios. And there I was, a girl from the hood of Sacramento with only two test shoots by a little-known San Francisco photographer. I was beyond intimidated, but it couldn't dampen my excitement—once the drugs had worn off.

Making friends was never difficult for me, and I quickly bonded with the girls. By the end of my first week, I was dancing the night away with my new roomies at Bains Douches, the absolute hottest club in Paris at the time. It was the beginning of six amazing years when I traveled the world, danced with princes, and spent evenings with some of the most interesting people at some of the most lavish parties one could ever imagine.

Not to go all *Eat Pray Love*, but traveling can be wonderfully therapeutic. During those years, I wasn't necessarily overcoming any particular hardship, but the experiences gifted me a sense of awareness that proved helpful during my breakup and subsequent early midlife crisis. Plus, it afforded me a wonderful life. I made good money and paid back my parents all they had lent me through the years. Looking back, I cherish the time I spent there and would never change a single minute. I was introduced to so many amazing cultures, languages, and, of course, so much delicious food (besides French).

If you haven't traveled, I suggest you go immediately to Milan and head to the Duomo, a beautiful church in the center of the city. When you get there, find the little hole-in-the-wall sandwich shop and order a mozzarella-and-*pomodoro* sandwich. *Molto molto caldo!* (Very, very hot!) Enjoy. #CarbsRock.

One day, I'm going to take my entire family to Milan . . . and Sardinia and Saint-Tropez. We'll of course travel by private plane and stay on my überluxurious yacht. Hey, a girl can dream, can't she?

While I'll never regret my decision to move abroad, I did learn firsthand the importance of a college education. I would never force my children into doing anything, but I will encourage them to pursue an advanced degree in whatever field they choose. My oldest son currently wants to be a veterinarian—which requires years of schooling. My younger son wants to be a gangsta rapper, so either I send him to Compton High

School or maybe suggest a dual major in music and theater? I haven't quite figured that one out yet. Perhaps "bonus mom" can help him with his music career? #GoodForSomething.

Six years after I moved to Europe, I came back to Los Angeles to shoot a Coors Light commercial and ended up at an obnoxious nightclub called Grandville on Santa Monica Boulevard in West Hollywood. Across the bar, I spotted an insanely attractive Cuban man who just couldn't keep his eyes off me, and I couldn't keep my eyes off him either. It was love at first sight—or, perhaps, lust. Yes, we slept together that first night. I would never endorse sleeping with someone you just met, because half of the fun is the challenge. But, man, was it fucking hot! I used to joke that he "raped" me. Rape jokes are never funny, except when they are. I was saying, "No, no, no," the entire time, but we all know that despite the adage, sometimes no *does* mean yes.

That was the night I met my future ex-husband. Not long after, we were in a fully committed relationship. Unlike with Joey, when Eddie asked me to stay in Los Angeles, I said yes. He didn't want me traveling anymore, he wanted me by his side at all times, and I was more than happy to oblige. I adored how protective he was of me. We moved in together and were crazy in love. #BeyonceSaidItBest. I would have done anything for that man. (I would also like to point out that #BeyonceSaidItBest again when she sang "to the left, to the left.")

Five years later, we were married at the Ritz Carlton in Laguna Niguel, California, and I decided to forgo traveling for modeling entirely. My husband wanted to start a family pretty quickly after our wedding, and he wanted the little wife at home to raise the kids, clean the house, and cook the meals. He was traditional in that respect (one of his few conservative qualities), so that's what I did—with the help of a nanny, two in-laws, and a housekeeper. After I got pregnant with our first son, I largely scaled back on modeling, but booked the occasional shoot just as a way to stay social and catch up with friends. He was making a good enough living that we didn't need the extra income. Plus, I felt that I had already lived a full life, so I was thoroughly content being a kept woman and more than happy to step aside and let my husband enjoy the spotlight.

I had yet to learn that while there's nothing wrong

with elevating your partner, that should not come at the cost of your own identity. I lost myself in my relationship. It's an easy thing to do and a mistake I will never make again. No one person is exactly the same as the year before or even a week before, but when we're blinded by love, we don't always make the smartest choices for our own best interests. How could I be the best partner, friend, daughter, wife, or mother, if I was sidelining my own identity? The answer is, I couldn't. I will never take total responsibility for what happened in my divorce, but I will take responsibility for what I allowed to happen to *me*. During my marriage, I lost my voice. Before it, I was always opinionated, outspoken, and filter-free, but that faded over the years. I allowed myself to forget my self-worth.

When my new reality came to light, my life as a soon-to-be divorcée came as an extreme adjustment. I had stopped doing anything for myself. I no longer felt like an individual because for thirteen years, I was one-half of a "we." My ex-husband clearly didn't have that same dilemma. #JustSayin.

So when Eddie had left me with a shell of my former lifestyle and virtually no money—despite promising me that I would always be taken care of—I had no career to fall back on and no education to speak of.

I decided it was time to "do me." Around the time of my separation, the ghetto girl in me totally identified with a Drake song called "Over (I'm Doin' Me)." When you split up with someone, music can either save you or totally destroy you. I couldn't listen to the radio without hearing heartbreaking, sappy love songs that would drive me to tears. They were just everywhere, so I listened to this Drake song over and over: "What am I doin'? Oh, yeah, that's right, I'm doin' me!"

My modeling days were behind me, and I was without any other professional skill set. I was desperate to maintain some semblance of my former lifestyle—not for me, but for my children, who had grown accustomed to certain things. So much was already changing in their worlds that I wanted this transition to be as smooth as possible. And I needed a bit of that balance for my own sanity, as well. I knew I needed to make something of myself, but what was I going to do? I was thirty-six and well past my prime modeling years, so I figured that keeping my name in the press would eventually lead to some opportunities down the line. I even hired a publicist to give me some direction when dealing with the ever-present media and possibly to help develop opportunities to make some money. I knew that staying relevant was going to be important, and I refused to look like a doormat in the press. So when a tabloid reporter called to get a quote about Eddie's parenting skills, I fired off the first thought that came to my mind—and those who know me well know that's usually a terrible idea, but they also know that I am being brutally honest.

In a short time, my life had become a comedy of errors—except nothing about it was actually funny. I was incapable of catching any kind of break. A few days later, I was standing in the checkout line with my kids at the Albertsons in Calabasas, and staring back at me was a fresh batch of glossy magazines. I flipped through the pages until I came across an item about Eddie, and my heart sank. My slicing words were in big, bold letters: "Eddie Cibrian Is an Absentee Father." I was a better person than that, but I was holding on to so much anger. I guess it shouldn't have come as a huge shocker when my credit card—the only card that I had—was declined moments later. At first, I figured it had to be some kind of mistake. Maybe the strip was just bare (I had been doing my fair share of retail therapy), so I asked the cashier to call the bank and find out the problem. Apparently, the primary cardholder, Eddie, had canceled my access to the account. I could have died of embarrassment. There I was with a basket full of diapers, kid food, groceries, and sauvignon blanc—about $500 worth of stuff already bagged up—and a growing line of grouchy shoppers behind me waiting to check out.

I did the first thing that came to mind: I burst into tears, grabbed the boys, and headed toward the exit, leaving my cart and my dignity behind.

I knew in that moment that I would never be able to rely on Eddie again—the man who had promised to take care of me for the rest of my life. My spousal support was embarrassingly low, and I didn't have a job. I guess I shouldn't have been that surprised, since this was the same man who canceled my health insurance without even giving me the courtesy of a heads-up. (Cut to an expensive ankle injury that I'm still paying off.) Not to mention, I will be paying for the HPV for the rest of my life. Every three months, I am required to see my gynecologist for a checkup, and I have had two additional loop electrosurgical excision procedures (LEEPs) since my divorce. #TheGiftThatKeepsOnGiving.

I was forced to make some concessions. First things first: I needed a car, but who would lease a car to an unemployed single mother with zero credit? With my tail between my legs, I picked up the phone and called the one man I never wanted to burden but knew I could always depend on: my dad. Without hesitation, my parents agreed to cosign on a car for me: a Range Rover Sport. (Listen, I wasn't about to forgo all my former luxuries, but the Sport was far more cost-effective than a traditional Range Rover. I considered the downgrade my concession. Baby steps, people.) I was a jobless, homeless mother of two living out of her $1,200-a-month SUV and couch-surfing from one hospitable friend to the next. To add insult to serious injury, I also developed a nervous twitch in my left eye. #NotHot.

One of my closest friends actually suggested that I become an exotic dancer. She couched it by saying that since I might be too old to make a consistent living modeling, I should at least make some money off my great ass. I had already taken a few classes at Sheila Kelley's

S Factor, so while I wasn't a professional, I could easily find my way around a pole. Plus, if I found a strip club deep enough in the Valley, no one would ever know. This was coming from one of my most conservative friends, so I thought, "Oh, shit, if she's suggesting this, I'm in some big-ass trouble."

I must admit that I didn't immediately discard the idea. I've been to Valley strip clubs; I was pretty certain I could do fairly well. But I quickly realized that this divorce was already stripping me of most of my pride and self-respect anyway, so I might as well keep the little that I had remaining.

It was time to get creative. Besides becoming a stripper, how the fuck was I going to feed my babies? Our house in Calabasas had sold by now, but Eddie was holding the escrow funds ransom until I would agree to sign the horrid divorce agreement. Some people would call that blackmail, and some people are fucking lawyers. I can't reveal much about our settlement because it's strictly confidential, but what I can tell you is that it sucks fucking balls—gross balls. Be aware that if you're going through a divorce and your ex has shacked up with someone wealthy and therefore isn't pressured to find actual work, his swanky new lifestyle has zero effect on how much alimony you receive. I could understand why it was difficult for him to find time to audition when he spent most days frolicking on the beach in Mexico or going to the gym without his wedding ring on. (I mean, it's a demanding life.) Seriously though, the only other actor I see vacationing more than my ex-husband is George Clooney, but he was smart enough to never get married again. If my ex-husband allegedly can't find a job— regardless of the lifestyle he leads himself—I'm struggling to make ends meet, since he has virtually no income.

As much as it would please me to go into every sordid detail and reveal just how big of an asshole he could be, my lips are sealed. I had to sign away my right to speak about our divorce settlement in order to get the escrow funds from our Calabasas home, which put a roof over my head and gave the children and me a place to call home. In Eddie's defense (and in one of the few occasions I will ever defend this man), he was prepared to be generous to the boys and me while he still had a job on CBS's *CSI: Miami*. But once he was fired from the series, the game changed entirely. He assumed the firestorm surrounding our divorce was the reason Eddie wasn't asked to return to the show. I'm sure it had absolutely nothing to do with the fact that he can't actually act. Right. That makes total fucking sense. #Oblivious.

After our negotiations went south, so did my alimony and child-support checks. Ladies and gays, if you do plan to get married, don't marry a fucking actor. When Eddie was cast on NBC's *Playboy Club*, people assumed that I wanted his show to fail, but that couldn't be further from the truth. A well-paid and happy Eddie translated into a well-paid and happy Brandi. I needed him to work. I never watched the show, but I wanted it to succeed. Much like our marriage, it failed—and so I needed a job.

Driving around the city, it's clear that most people in Los Angeles don't have real jobs. At any hour of the day, the 405 freeway is completely jammed—for no reason. Even if it's 11:00 a.m. on a Wednesday, you're hard-pressed to find a table at Joan's on Third in West Hollywood or an elliptical machine at the Equinox in Beverly Hills. How were these people paying their rent, and how could I get in on it? I needed some income . . . and fast.

After my first few debacles dealing with the invasive world of tabloid magazines, I decided that if I wanted

Eddie to keep my credit cards activated, I needed to stay quiet. Immediately, I stopped taking calls from reporters looking for comments. But they were relentless—and as we all know, I have a pretty big mouth and a temper to match. You can't unspill the milk, and I had dumped out enough to fill a swimming pool. I turned off my phone, blocked numbers, and texted, "No comment." The quieter I became, the more they wanted to hear from me. It's like any relationship really: the more you ignore someone, the more that person wants you. And I guess there aren't too many "tabloid stars" that are willing to speak out publicly about their former spouses or their new girlfriends.

Not long after I went radio silent, my publicist started receiving offers from different media outlets to actually pay me for interviews. It was sort of laughable. I thought, "People will actually pay me to talk?" I'd been running my mouth since I uttered my first word, and now someone wanted to give me money for my opinion? It was genius—and proved lucrative. I didn't want to go out into the world and bash my ex-husband. With all of his over-the-top, superproduced public displays with LeAnn, he was doing a pretty good job of making himself look like an ass. But I also had a mounting stack of bills. I knew that the credit card company would eventually deactivate my card permanently. If he were smarter, he would have paid me well to shut the fuck up forever, as it appears LeAnn did with her ex-husband. (But then again, if that had happened for me, you wouldn't be reading this book! #JustSayin)

It turns out that I had supporters out there in the world: men and women who picked up these magazines and read these blogs who related to what I was going through and were interested in what I had to say. I had been told for so long that my ideas and opinions were foolish or stupid that I'd actually started believing it. Once I realized I had this wonderful following, I began getting opportunities to make appearances—and again, people would actually pay me to come to their party, store, or nightclub. My first paid appearance was for a "Fabulous and Single" party at a Las Vegas nightclub that my friend Deb Grimmel set up. She was working public relations for the Tao/Lavo Group and asked me if I was interested in hosting this event for her. I wasn't that well-known at the time, so I'm pretty sure she asked me mainly because we were friends, but I felt special and was extremely grateful. I could come out with a group of girlfriends, and they would put us up at the Venetian hotel and resort. The more appearances I did, the more I would stay press-relevant.

These small opportunities began piling up—$10,000 here and $10,000 there—and after a few months of capitalizing on some of them, I was finally able to lease a single-family home in Encino for my boys and me to live in. It was one of the first adult decisions that I had made completely on my own, and it felt amazing. With the help of my parents and the small amount of savings I did receive in my separation, I was finally able to start to build my own credit (which I'm still working on), pay my own bills, and figure out a way to get by from month to month. It was insanely gratifying. I'm not necessarily proud of the means I used, but I'm not ashamed of my actions either. It wasn't ideal, but I did what I had to in order to make ends meet, given the options available. It was also a hell of a lot better than stripping—I wanted to keep my evenings free to start dating again.

I discovered that my strongest skill is my voice. I'm honest, filter-free, and incapable of bullshitting—and that's apparently uncommon in Hollywood. For years,

I was told that what I thought and said didn't matter, so it took me a while to accept that people actually valued my opinions and that eventually I could look to offer them professionally. Going through my divorce, I was able to connect with other men and women, mostly via social-networking sites, who were going through similar and not-so-similar situations: marital problems, failed friendships, raising children, dieting, etc.

If someone had told me four years ago that I would be a cast member on Bravo's *Real Housewives* franchise and writing a book about breakup blunders and overcoming adversity, I would have laughed in his or her face. I was guilty of setting my own limitations. That's often the case when you've been in a relationship that made you question yourself. Or if you discover your partner fucked half the neighborhood.

When my life took an unimaginable turn, I was completely unprepared. While I was sure of handful of things—I could rock the smallest bikini, fuck like a rock star, and make a homemade penne Bolognese that would change your life—I was insecure about my actual abilities to make a living. It can still feel a bit surreal at times. If you learn anything from my journey, it's that sometimes the best opportunities are not only unexpected, they may come in the most unusual forms—perhaps a reality show focusing on the teenage drama of six middle-aged women, or becoming the victim of a staged photo opportunity at your five-year-old's soccer game with his new stepmom. Perhaps.

I had managed to find a way to pay the necessary bills while still being able to purchase indecent, luxury lingerie to wear for a boyfriend I didn't have. My alimony expired toward the end of 2012, and Eddie now only provides me with child support, but I have my own job, and I'm making my own money. I got the last laugh, because I knew I was going to be okay.

brandi's babble

Overindulgence can be a good thing—especially when it teaches you what you don't need.

CHAPTER **FOUR**

With Friends like These . . .

There are two truths when it comes to girlfriends: they can be the absolute best and they can be the absolute worst. (Most of mine are just about the bestest ever, though.) There's no other way to slice it. Remember when you and your very best friend in the fourth grade painstakingly coordinated your outfits for "Twins Day" at school? Fast-forward to high school when the same girl threatened to kick your ass for getting a haircut that too closely resembled hers. Remember when you spent an entire weekend on the couch with your best friend eating ice cream and watching *Zoolander*, because she was nursing her first real heartbreak? Fast-forward to a few months later, when the same friend begged you to go to the pharmacy to pick up her Valtrex prescription because she's too embarrassed. So, I repeat, girls are both the best and the worst.

If nothing else, a breakup is an opportunity to weed out the total users in your life from your real friends. This is especially true in Hollywood, where people can smell the spotlight a mile away and will ride your coattails all the way down the Pacific Coast Highway, if you let them. LA hangers-on are about as common as Botox and second wives. Although, this theory can be applied to friendships regardless of where you live. If you have more of something—whether it's money, power, fame, or happiness—some people around you will be jealous of you and resentful for it. Occasionally, it's natural to totally obsess over your best friend's new Alexander McQueen skull clutch or the amazing new promotion she got at work; even the best of friends are guilty of it. The difference is, if you're a good friend, you can be totally envious of her fabulous purchase or his new job, but also be genuinely happy for him or her. Unfortunately, in La La Land, those kinds of "real" friends are few and far between.

That's my experience, at least.

* * *

I had it all. I had the hot husband who had somehow managed to develop a modicum of celebrity. I had a beautiful six-bedroom home in Calabasas and was a stay-at-home mom with two gorgeous little boys. I had wonderful friends who were there for me at the drop of a hat. I had a limitless credit card and a husband who never questioned a single bill. I thought I had won the life lottery.

Apparently, so did my friends, many of whom were struggling with their own relationships and careers. I'll be completely honest: a glimpse of fame can be incredibly intoxicating if you've never experienced it before. Even though Eddie wasn't well-known, being a working "actor" came with its fair share of perks, and in our social circle he was the only one who had established any kind of name for himself in the industry.

There is no exact science to why some people "make it" and others don't. It's perseverance and hard work coupled with an obscene amount of luck. I've said it before: Eddie is a pretty face, not a talented actor. That's not to say he couldn't be. If he spent half as much time learning to develop his craft as he did juggling all the women in his life, he'd probably have a shelf full of Oscars—or at least a few Emmys.

Once Eddie started carving out a television career for himself, it was amazing how many people came out of the woodwork. But I loved it. I loved being the woman who had it all. And I loved being the woman behind that man. When we were married, we had a wealth of friends who seemed so present and supportive. I felt so blessed.

As the saying goes, the higher the climb, the bigger the fall.

When my world began crumbling around me, I realized I had three tiers of friendship:

1. Those friends who hit the road at the first sign of trouble. It's all gravy when you're throwing parties with top-shelf booze or picking up the tab at the hottest new restaurant, but when you actually need a hand? Forget it.

2. Those who stick around long enough just to see you miserable before jumping on the next rising star (in this case, LeAnn). It's actually twisted. You allow these people into

your world and share countless memories with them, but you learn one day that they resented you all along. And when you are at your lowest of lows, they rejoice in your misery, because they have seemingly been waiting for this moment. I guess that makes people feel better about their own lives. Then one day, they're just gone.

3. Those who won't budge. Friends for life. These are the men and women that I cherish. Come rain or storm, we will always be there for one another. Maybe that's the silver lining after having to deal with shitty people: you can truly appreciate the good ones.

If you had asked me four years ago, I would have been certain that almost all of my friends would fall into the third category. I would have bet my life on it. Being seriously wrong was something I was getting used to by now.

Turns out about half of my friends snuggled right into the first two slots. That revelation was almost as heartbreaking as my divorce.

* * *

I wasn't the first of my friends to go through a divorce, and odds are, I won't be the last. One friend in particular went through a messy, nasty divorce just a few years before Eddie and I separated. She was Asian, a stylist I met while modeling, but we didn't hang out much until we were both retired, pregnant, and living in the same city for once. Originally, our friendship was built out of convenience from being on the same jobs, but it eventually developed into something I valued. So when she told me she and her husband were getting a divorce, I was happy to be a part of her support system. I even moved her into my guest bedroom during her darker days. I would spend countless hours doubling as her therapist over bottles of wine and leisurely lunches—but unlike traditional therapy sessions, I always paid the check at the end. I didn't mind, because that's what friends are for. Money was going to be tight for her for a while, and I was certain that she would be there for me if I ever needed her.

And she was . . . for a price.

When I decided to check into the Beverly Hills Hotel

(after discovering Eddie's second affair), she immediately packed a bag and came along with me. And why wouldn't she? She knew I was hitting rock-bottom and that I needed her. I assumed that since she had already been down this path, she would be the rock to help me figure out this new life and repay the kindness I had shown her. I'm sure it had nothing to do with a free stay at one of the most luxurious hotels in Los Angeles or the chance to see a former trophy wife fall from her pedestal. She sat there, wiped away my tears, and told me how much better off I would be without him. She also ordered an insanely expensive bottle of tequila and put it on my room tab.

She wasn't perfect, but she was there. What I did discover was that having a recent divorcée as a "friend" meant that I also had a round-the-clock drinking partner, if I needed one. Like me, she was single, unattached, and seriously enjoying her freedom for the first time in years—something I found attractive in friends at the time. After her divorce, she slept around and was always eager to drown her sorrows on my dime. However, that was the extent of what she could offer. It was a one-way street, and if I wasn't going in the same direction,

I needed to get out of the fucking lane. Otherwise, she would run my ass over.

She quickly grew tired of listening to my problems and rarely had the time to listen to me vent or cry. She was always down for a good time, but never a sad time. After all the meals I had picked up, she never offered to pick up a tab or even give me the courtesy of a half-hearted wallet reach—despite knowing the severity of my financial crisis. Although, at a Sunday BBQ in the Valley, she did once offer me the opportunity to be in a threesome with a really gorgeous firefighter she was dating. Unfortunately, I already had other plans.

I wanted to give her the benefit of the doubt. I figured that her inability to listen to my problems was just self-preservation. Maybe it was hard for her to witness my divorce? Maybe it was, in a strange way, forcing her to relive her own heartbreak (although she also confided in me that she married for money and not for love)? I started to back off our friendship, because I didn't need to get trapped in her downward spiral. I wasn't trying to abandon her; I was just trying to protect myself. Much as I was with Eddie, I was completely blindsided when the floor fell out from underneath me.

It turns out I should have listened to my gut: she was a selfish asshole and extremely unhealthy for me to be around. About two years later, she sold a completely false and insanely hurtful story about me to a tabloid, to make some extra cash. Times were not that tough for her, so she chose to be cruel purely for the sake of hurting me. #JustSayin.

Once you realize that a friend is only looking out for himself or herself, you need to be able to cut your losses and walk away. A tiger doesn't change its stripes. If you're going through a breakup, the idea of saying good-bye to a friend isn't the greatest feeling, but it's for the best in the long run. There's already so much negativity in the world, why keep the door open for more? Like they say: Fool me once, shame on you; fool me twice, go fuck yourself. Or maybe that's just me who says that.

During the divorce of yet another close friend, I was by her side for the entire roller coaster and, again, moved her into my guest room. (I should have started renting that place out by the night.) Unlike my stylist friend, this was a girl I grew up with. We met in Europe as teenagers and traveled the world together—we even had our first threesome together! We were as close as any two friends could be. Eventually, we both moved back to LA and met our future husbands—who also became great friends. We were bridesmaids in each other's weddings and spent most weekends together. It couldn't have worked out better if we had planned it, except that we both married fucking douche bags.

When I was having dark moments, she tried to be there for me the best she could, but she was still struggling herself. One night she tried to take me to Shamrock on Sunset Boulevard to get my first tattoo, telling me it would be the first step on the road to self-discovery. I considered getting just a little heart someplace private. I'd never considered it before, so I got two steps inside the tattoo parlor before my better judgment kicked in: MILFs don't have ink.

She was my sister in a lot of ways, but I could sense a growing distance between us over time. Months went by, and she became increasingly unavailable—to talk, to work out, and even to party (which was a rarity for my group of girlfriends). I was totally baffled, but she promised me nothing was wrong.

Shortly after, it all made sense.

One afternoon, a mutual friend sent me an e-mail with a link to paparazzi photos. I opened the link and got my breath knocked out of me. Staring back at me from the computer screen was my best friend of more than fifteen years walking down the street and laughing with my husband's new wife. I leaned in closer to the screen, certain I wasn't seeing this correctly.

Why would my friend for nearly half my life be hanging out with my ex-husband's new wife? The woman who sat by my side during some of my darkest hours was now parading around town with the same woman who caused me all that pain. With shaky hands, I fumbled through my purse for my cell phone, flipped it open, and dialed her number. There was no answer. She had to have known I would figure all of this out eventually, even though these photographs were "oh so candid."

When we finally spoke, she had an excuse for everything. She had been a bit distant because she was trying to work things out with her ex-husband. She assumed that would be difficult for me to deal with, seeing as I was still struggling with my own divorce. As for LeAnn, well, my friend's ex-husband and Eddie remained friends after both of our divorces and were hanging out a lot (translation: hitting on cocktail waitresses). Her ex had asked her to spend time with LeAnn as a part of their reconciliation, so my friend agreed. She swore to me that she only did it to pacify her ex-husband, and "it didn't mean anything."

"Hmm, I've already heard that line from Eddie," I thought, not interested in the bullshit she was trying to sell me. Even if you were pointing a gun at my head, you could never force me to sit in the same room with my best friend's homewrecker, and I sure as hell wasn't going for fucking iced lattes and shopping sprees with her.

How could my friend do that to me? I was absolutely beside myself that she was willing to throw away our decades-long friendship just for the opportunity to be the background girl in all of LeAnn's paparazzi shots. Was having your photo taken that important? I knew that in the back of her head she had always thought that she should be famous, but, really? I guess friends really are a dime a dozen.

As much as I hold my friend accountable for the

demise of our relationship, in the back of my head I knew this was somehow LeAnn's doing. She had everything else in my life, so why wouldn't she want all my friends? It's not like she ever had any of her own—child stars rarely do. By this point, most of the magazines and blogs were referring to her as a "Brandi clone," so I guess it makes sense that she wanted to completely inhabit my world. I wonder when she'll ask everyone to start calling her B and start trying to come to Sacramento for holidays. #StalkerMuch?

Unfortunately, this wasn't the only one of my "friends" to be lured over to the dark side. It was mostly the wives and girlfriends of Eddie's buddies whom I had developed close relationships with. Eventually, I spotted most of them somewhere on the blogosphere—at one time or another—walking along the sand in Laguna Beach or snowsuit shopping in Aspen with my husband's new wife.

While I have an arsenal of terrible names I could call LeAnn, *stupid* isn't one of them. This country-music singer was clever. To make Eddie's transition as smooth as possible from wife number one to wife number two, she totally inhabited his world—or at least what he wanted his world to be. She must have figured that befriending these women would be the easiest way to keep Eddie comfortable. (Plus, she can't stand it when anyone dislikes her. I guess she'll have to get used to that.) She wooed them with an all-expense-paid vacation to Cabo San Lucas—complete with private planes, private beaches, and private chefs—and the unspoken promise that their own stars might rise if they stood next to her long enough. After all, there's a photographer lurking around every corner, right? (Usually because she's called them.)

Losing these women was a blessing in disguise. Their absence allowed me to fully appreciate the handful of extremely loyal friends who have stuck by my side throughout this journey. These are the men and women who understand me better than I sometimes understand myself. They knew when I needed them nearby, they knew when I needed space, and they knew to lift me out of the hole I was digging for myself when I started losing control.

However, even my best friends didn't know how to deal with the overwhelming amount of media surrounding my divorce. I didn't, either. It was unlike any breakup any of us had experienced. For months, the coverage was incessant. Then it would die down until something happened to reignite the fire: Eddie and LeAnn's moving in together, my DUI charge, Eddie and LeAnn's wedding, my new role on *Real Housewives of Beverly Hills*. The constant reminders of the affair that ultimately led to Eddie's and my divorce made moving on more challenging than it would be for the average divorcée, and my friends were unsure of how to handle it when they came across something on the Internet or in a magazine.

It was the million-dollar question for today's world of tabloid-celebrity breakups: What do you do when you see paparazzi photos of your friend's ex with his or her new partner? It's the same predicament people nowadays encounter through social media. Do you tell your friend when you see photos of her ex-husband walking along the beach with his new wife and the kids? Do you send them to her? She probably doesn't want to see, but you'd rather she learn about it from you than be blindsided later. Or do you ignore it? It's never fun being the bearer of bad news, so perhaps you just let someone else spill the beans?

During the early, obsessive days of my divorce, I was desperate for any information I could get on Eddie and LeAnn. When a friend would send me a Twitter photo of bonus mom cuddling with my kids, I would stare at it for hours. I was hungry for any information I could get my hands on, but those were my virtual-cutting days. Today, I'd rather not know about it. (I believe that's what my therapist calls "progress.") I don't need a friend to send me a photo of my ex-husband's replacement wife in a bikini, even if only to point out her stretch marks. I know my friends are just trying to make me laugh or prove how loyal they are to me, but all it does is remind me that he chose her—stretch marks and all. Despite my offering him a second chance and all his promises of fidelity, he wouldn't let go of LeAnn, and our family was destroyed because of it.

I understand that my life has forever been changed by their decisions and, for better or for worse, they will be a chapter in my life—one that I will occasionally need to relive, whether it's in writing this book, discussing it with friends or viewers of *Real Housewives of Beverly Hills* going through difficult times, or in the conversations I will one day need to have with my sons and whomever I choose to share my life with.

However, I no longer have Google alerts set to notify me when Eddie and LeAnn stage another paparazzi shoot at my son's soccer game, and I don't need to be reminded that they will soon be celebrating their second wedding anniversary. (Really, they had to get married in fucking Malibu? #BlowMe) And I no longer need the daily updates from my friends. I know they think an "update" is what I prefer, but it's not. Not anymore.

So, unless it's something that is essential for your friend to know, spare him or her the details. While those friends might be angry when they first find out you withheld information, eventually they will understand that you did it with their best interests at heart.

Rest assured that if your friend wants to vent about some obnoxious article or Facebook post, or if he or she is teary-eyed and needs a shoulder, he or she will reach out.

As the divorcée or subject of the breakup, depending on your friends is absolutely crucial, but know your limits! Friends can quickly grow tired of feeling sorry for you—unless you're always picking up the check, in which case their sympathies (and wineglasses) are bottomless.

People, hopefully, have their own lives to live and their own problems to worry about. It's easy to become completely self-involved when you're faced with hardships, but it's important to remember to be there for your friends, too. You have to be able to read the signs. When they no longer pick up on the first ring (and perhaps not at all) or when their responses and advice become less sympathetic, it's time to reevaluate how much you're leaning on a particular person. It's not because these people don't love you, it's because they have their own shit going on (or they've been abducted by LeAnn Rimes). While sometimes we all need to climb out of our own fog to realize that we're far from perfect, what I can say with total confidence is that I've always been a good friend.

It may seem obvious, but when you're going through any difficult period, spending time with those who know and love you can be tremendously healing. It's not always about curling up on the couch with a box of Kleenex and a pint of ice cream. Being around your friends provides a great opportunity to get back to being you. While we may feel this overwhelming urge to flee, we know running isn't going to help. Wherever you go, your problems will follow, because it's impossible to check your brain or your heart at the border. They will follow you anywhere you go.

I chose to surround myself with either people who made me laugh or those I could drown my sorrows with. Laughter can cure just about anything—except a wretched hangover. For that, I suggest EBOOST.

After countless tears, laughs, and memories, you learn that your friends will always be there for you. Unless your ex's new wife takes them to Cabo.

brandi's **babble**

There are two kinds of friends to avoid at all costs: wannabes and former child stars.

CHAPTER FIVE

Drugs and Other Drugs

Shortly after giving birth to my youngest, sitting on the floor of the Woodland Hills Target's diaper aisle and crying was fast becoming a part of my daily routine. Now, I'm not a doctor, but I'm pretty sure this was indicative of a serious problem.

After Jake was born, I would find any reason to get out of the house and spend hours wandering around somewhere aimlessly. With a newborn and a four-year-old at home, I felt I was losing my mind, and I was in desperate need of some support. While some people go to church for spiritual guidance, I sought the comfort of my favorite superstore. Like clockwork every afternoon, I would announce to the nanny that we were out of diapers or hand wash or toilet paper or whatever most quickly came to mind. (Not that she understood anything that I was saying, since she only spoke Spanish. I suppose I was trying to convince myself.) Without bothering to put on makeup, brush my teeth, or even get out of my pajamas, I would grab the car keys and hightail it to the driveway. As soon as my Range Rover hit the Target parking lot, I would start to cry, feeling some inexplicable sense of relief. Target became my little sanctuary where I would roam up and down the aisles with my Starbucks, looking at picture frames, flipping through magazines, and trying on costume jewelry. But as soon as I caught a glimpse of myself in one of the hundreds of mirrors in Target, I would burst into tears. I didn't even recognize myself anymore: a thirty-four-year-old Valley housewife with two kids, puffy eyes, leftover baby weight, and a nest of blond hair. Some days, I didn't even need the mirror to burst into tears. I would turn down the diaper aisle and guilt would wash over me, then the fear and the waterworks would come until I could calm down and get back to shopping. So it went for most afternoons for the better part of a month. The staff quickly got used to seeing the crazy crying lady loitering in the aisles and, after a few days, stopped asking if everything was okay (but I usually bought something so I didn't feel completely weird coming back the next day). I was like an unofficial door greeter, except instead of welcoming customers to the store, I scared the shit out of them.

It didn't take a PhD (or even a GED) to figure out that I had developed a pretty wicked case of the baby blues, but it took me a while to recognize it in myself. If I were standing on the outside, I'm sure I would easily have recognized it, but during those few weeks I was in a cloud and fairly incapable of rational thought. I mean, hello, I was spending most of my afternoons in a Target—a lot of times I didn't even bother pushing a cart.

"What did you do today?" Eddie would ask on the days he actually came home from work at a reasonable hour.

"I went to Target again and cried," I would respond nonchalantly. At the time, this sounded to me like a totally normal response. It was, in fact, what I did that day. I could tell that Eddie was concerned about my mental health, so I told him it was normal. I think we can all agree it was not fucking normal. #CuckooForCocoaPuffs.

While my depression was considerable, it never

reached a psychotic state where I wanted to cause any physical harm to my children or myself. I thought this was just a normal hormonal roller coaster that would eventually pass after my body settled back down.

After weeks of my feeling totally desperate, crying for no reason, and with a purse filled with Target credit-card receipts, Eddie finally suggested I see someone about getting a prescription to help with the transition. I knew he was concerned, and I am grateful to him for that, but I needed to come that realization on my own.

Then, I snapped.

I could hear my baby screaming down the hall while I was trying to get Mason dressed for the day. Frustration was mounting in my voice as I tried to manage my giggly four-year-old, who was grasping for a nearby toy. He was having a little bit of a tough time adjusting to having a new baby in the house and just trying to understand the change. We all were; newborns are an adjustment (even though the first two months is when they spend most of the day sleeping and you can tote them around just about anywhere!).

DRINKING **and** TWEETING

When I turned to grab Mason's shirt off the dresser, he tried wandering away, as toddlers tend to do. That's when I lost it. I grabbed the waist of his pants, yanked him around to face me, and screamed, "Come. Fucking. On!"

Seeing the total fear in his eyes was all the motivation I needed to make a change. My poor little four-year-old was terrified of his mommy, the one person who should always make him feel safe. His eyes filled up with tears and my heart sank. I grabbed his little body and pulled him into my chest. "Mommy's sorry," I told him. "Mommy made a mistake. I'm sorry. I won't yell at you like that again. I promise." I felt absolutely horrible, and it's a moment I will never forget. It was scarring for me, and I realized that I never wanted to react that way again toward my children, as long as I lived.

That was the final straw. Something was really wrong with me, and I needed to go talk to someone.

That's when I finally told Eddie, "I'm not happy. I screamed at Mason for no reason. I think I need help now." He encouraged me to set up an appointment with my gynecologist that week. At the time, the world had just witnessed in the media the Brooke Shields–Tom Cruise war of words on postpartum depression, and the disorder had a negative connotation. The public seemed fiercely divided on the topic, but it seemed silly to me that anyone would ever believe a man over a woman in that situation. How many times had Tom Cruise gone into labor? How many times had he had to wake up in the middle of the night to breast-feed? How often did he have crazy female hormones pumping through his body? To this day, if any man wants to sit on his high horse and judge women who choose to vocalize their struggles, I say, "Go fuck yourself."

A man can never understand what it's like to go through childbirth. It is both the most rewarding and most terrifying experience you can imagine. For the rest of my life, I will cherish the moments I brought each of my sons into the world, but I also know I never want to go through that experience again. So, when it comes down to Brooke versus Tom, I'm going to side with the woman every single time.

Brooke's candor about her postpartum depression also served as a huge wake-up call to mothers that they were not alone. Before then, people weren't vocal about the baby blues, so women suffered behind closed doors.

Today, women are open about struggling after having a baby. Guess what? When you bring a newborn home from the hospital, it's not all cupcakes and rainbows. The first couple months are hard—actually, they sort of blow. And I had help! I envy those moms and dads who can do it on their own; I know I wouldn't have been able to make it without a support staff. I was never ashamed of it, because I knew it was a hormonal imbalance, and it didn't make me a bad mother. I would be a bad mom if I didn't get myself better. I think that if something is wrong and a pill can fix it, take the fucking pill. Life is way too short to spend your days miserable and taking your family for granted. (I'm still hoping for a pill that can turn me into a lesbian. The women in my life are amazing and fantastic partners, but when it comes to anything south of the border, I'm a strictly dickly kind of chick.)

"Listen, I'm going to Target and walking around aimlessly for hours, just to get out of the house," I told the doctor when I went to see her later that same week.

"I'm crying for absolutely no reason all the time. And worst of all, I'm yelling at my toddler for no apparent reason. I need help."

Immediately, my doctor recognized the signs and suggested I begin taking ten milligrams of Lexapro once a day, preferably in the morning. Within two weeks, I started noticing a tremendous change in my personality. I felt calm, balanced, and happy—three things I hadn't felt since before I went into labor. And probably not all at the same time since before I had Mason! It changed my life. I definitely noticed a lower sex drive, but that was okay for the time being. It was so high to begin with that I was fine with a temporary reprieve. Postpartum depression doesn't last forever. Once the baby starts smiling, laughing, and developing a personality of his or her own, it gets easier. My doctor and I decided on a program that would wean me off the medication within six months by lowering the doses systematically. By Jake's first birthday, I was off my happy pill and back to what I thought was my "normal" life.

That would soon change.

Roughly a year later, news broke of Eddie's affair with LeAnn—and it was just everywhere. I finally saw the video with my own eyes once I got back from Parrot Cay. I knew then that I was in for an emotional roller-coaster ride. Within about twenty-four hours, I determined that for me to have even the slightest chance of coming through this in one piece, I was going to need some help ASAP. I picked up the phone and called my doctor.

"Are you trembling?" she asked.

"I'm not okay," I said.

Sensing the sadness in my voice, she immediately sent a Lexapro prescription to my local CVS pharmacy.

Besides the love I have for my boys, I credit Lexapro for getting me through my divorce. People have criticized me for being open about my use of antidepressant and antianxiety drugs, wondering why I would admit to something like that. My response? Fuck you. There is nothing wrong with treating a neurochemical imbalance. In fact, I think it's negligent to ignore problems and hope that with enough sleep and a healthy diet they'll just go away. Bullshit. I'm hoping that my sharing my story will help another struggling mom out there—plus I never intend to give up Del Taco.

Pills aren't the answer to everyone's problems, and

prescription-drug dependencies are both real and scary. (I've seen enough *Intervention* to know this.) However, I found that Lexapro can offer me the stability I need to play soccer with my boys without breaking down in tears. It has been the crutch I sometimes need to be a good parent and to get through my days while actually enjoying them! This is simply my truth.

I don't know about other cities, but in Los Angeles about 90 percent of all women are either taking or have taken some kind of happy pill—and I know with certainty every single Valley housewife has a standing prescription. They don't call it the Valley Vitamin for nothing. A lot of my friends are on Lexapro—either because they're struggling with their role as a new mother and all the hormonal changes that come with it, or because they're simply getting older, and getting old sucks for everyone, especially for former models.

People act as if it were this dirty little secret. No one wants to talk about it, because it's like admitting some kind of failure. Men and women are far more comfortable talking openly about smoking pot or snorting cocaine than they are about needing the assistance of a legal antidepressant. It's like, "Hey, I'm just partying.

I don't need drugs to get through the day. I am in control of my days. I just do a bump or toke a bowl now and again because, unlike you, I'm totally normal." #Hypocrites.

I've talked openly about it both in interviews and on my Twitter feed. People shouldn't feel as if it were this terrible thing to recognize a problem, recognize that they're mistreating themselves and the people around them, and want to get help. As soon as I mention to people that I'm on Lexapro, they immediately launch into their own story about Zoloft or Prozac. I think people want to be honest about it, much as with postpartum depression, but still can't shake the stigma surrounding it. Hell, if I were afraid of what people might think, I'd never leave my house—or wear a bikini.

I'm also not afraid to admit that I occasionally rely on Xanax to help me with my anxiety. While most users of Lexapro require it daily, people require Xanax only during extremely stressfully situations. After the Lexapro, it was the very next prescription called in to my local pharmacy.

Xanax helps keep me calm when I feel a panic attack coming on—those usually occur during short flights on small airplanes (those of you who saw the second season of *Real Housewives of Beverly Hills* will get that reference) or on the morning you find out your ex-husband has married the woman he had an affair with, and your children walked her down the fucking aisle. #XanaxRules. While my now-small dosage of Lexapro grants me the sense of normalcy I need to get through the day, the Xanax mellows me out completely (and makes me a little silly). Like I said, it's not by any means a habit, and I'm definitely not operating any heavy machinery while under its influence, but it gets the job done when needed.

The one habit I did need to sideline was my drinking. After my divorce—even with the help of Lexapro—I fell into a bit of a tailspin (and an eventual DUI arrest). My life had become the textbook Cougar Diet: sauvignon blanc, Lexapro, and weekly magazines. Plus, the Lexapro (an antidepressant) coupled with the alcohol (a depressant) made for an extremely dangerous combination.

Ironically, I rarely drank when Eddie and I were

together. We'd have an occasional glass of wine with dinner and definitely loosen up at parties or events, but I wasn't a big drinker. That quickly changed after we separated. White wine became my constant shoulder to lean on. Coupled with the Lexapro, it was the only way I could get myself through my days and get to sleep at night. I realize how dangerous that was, but my life was unraveling at the seams.

So, you've all heard the story: I slashed the tires of my husband's two Harley-Davidsons. Not only is it true, I would do it again in a heartbeat. After two glasses of wine and a particularly bad evening, I had worked myself up enough to grab the largest knife out of the kitchen block and head straight to the garage. I slashed four tires in all—two wheels on two bikes. I'm not necessarily proud of my actions, but in that moment it felt really, really good. I was hurting so badly and made a knee-jerk decision to ruin something I knew he loved.

In my defense, I told Eddie what I had done before he tried to drive either of them. He wasn't too thrilled with my actions, but what was he going to do? Have an affair? Plus we were still married at the time, so I actually owned the bikes, too. Given everything he'd put me through, he was seriously lucky that's all I took a knife to. Don't think I didn't fantasize about going all Lorena Bobbitt on his ass.

I wasn't trying to kill him (not this day anyway); I just wanted to piss him off. #Success.

I don't blame the wine for sending me into a spiral. I wanted to do it anyway, but the wine gave me the courage.

Two glasses of white wine was enough for me to get tanked. Luckily, two glasses of wine is about all I can handle nowadays. However, for a long time it wasn't two glasses I needed to calm me down, it was two bottles. That much alcohol for a woman who weighs 120 pounds is extremely unhealthy. I'm pretty sure my organs are pickled.

Considering that I was simultaneously watching another woman fill my shoes entirely and completely take over my life (#SingleWhiteFemale), I'm pretty lucky that I didn't become a fucking crack whore or a heroin-addicted stripper. Well, the stripper option was briefly on the table, but heroin? Not a chance. I saw first-hand how that fucks people up. #Models.

I was drinking so profusely that the hideous hangovers actually stopped, so I started having booze-filled lunches. I started hosting my friends every night for man-bashing parties, so I didn't have to drink alone. I also became a pro at drunken sex-skyping with a handful of friends with benefits. (That's what the kids are calling it, right?) Clearly, these were all distractions so that I wouldn't be forced to deal with my problems and sadness.

Yes, drinking became a dependency, and I'm not proud of it. Sitting at soccer practice, I would watch the mounting e-mail exchanges between our lawyers, and the craving would hit me like a ton of bricks. I would pack up the kids as quickly as possible so Mommy could get back to the house and relax with a bottle of "grape juice." My trips to the grocery store became much more frequent, almost daily. I would make a beeline to the wine aisle and search for the already-refrigerated screw-tops. (I did not have time to bother with uncorking the damn things.) That's when I started to realize what a problem it was becoming. I seriously didn't want to waste time uncorking the fucking bottle?

While I regret my reliance on alcohol, I always to try to find a silver lining in any situation. Drinking became a way for me to socialize again. I spent months hiding out and feeling sorry for myself, only allowing those closest to me (or whom I thought were closest to me) into my world. One glass of wine alone could take the edge off, and I became more relaxed about reentering civilization. After two or three glasses of wine, my confidence was completely restored. Chardonnay—or any white wine—was a huge kick-starter to my ability to start dating again. At first, drunken sex was the only kind of sex I could have (especially because I wasn't necessarily attracted to my first boyfriend after my split). My grape-juice problem became my "rape"-juice problem. It took about two years before I could have sober sex. Actually, it took me about two years of overindulging in white wine before I could do most things sober, when it came to men. I think two years is a good barometer for anyone going through any kind of major change—whether it's divorce, death, illness, a new job, a new home, or a new relationship. After twenty-four months, most of the dust should have settled, and you can start moving on with your life in its current state. Or maybe I just made that up to make myself feel better. #WhateversClever.

I'm aware that it sounds as if I was an alcoholic. Maybe I was, but it wasn't the booze in itself that I was addicted to; it was the need to escape my problems. Once I mastered that, I was able to curb the drinking. It had a lot to do with therapy, but more to do with the humiliating DUI charge I was slapped with and the Breathalyzer I was required to install in my car for five months (you'll read about that stuff later).

Anyone who watches *Housewives* or keeps up with my Twitter feed knows that I still like my wine, but long gone are the nights when I would polish off two bottles. Today, two glasses is a big night, and I definitely feel it the next day. And I never drive buzzed.

brandi's **babble**

Take a fucking cab.

CHAPTER SIX

17 Again

Be honest. If you had the chance to have your seventeen-and-a-half-year-old pussy again, wouldn't you jump at the opportunity? That was my perfect pussy age. Virgin? No, too painful. And, let's be honest, a little awkward. Twenty-one? No, thanks. I had already spent too many years in Europe by that point. Seventeen and a half was my ideal.

These were my choices when I visited Beverly Hills–based vaginal-rejuvenation pioneer Dr. David Matlock. I never imagined myself looking into such a procedure. Don't get me wrong; I'm very pro-self-enhancement. For example, I always knew that I would get my boobs done after having children. (I seriously don't understand why women bother doing it before.) In the nineties, I would go to San Francisco to see one of the first plastic surgeons in the country to specialize in Botox. I started using cellulite cream as a twentysomething. I have never been coy about my vanity, I just never expected to find myself at Dr. Matlock's office—but my life's journey had shifted course, and I had decided to shift with it.

My ex-husband never practiced self-control, so it came as no surprise that he continued dating his new girlfriend while still living under the same roof as me. He would leave for days at a time without even the courtesy of a thinly veiled explanation (I wouldn't have believed his ass anyway, but I would have appreciated it if he at least had the decency to lie). We were separated, but hadn't yet moved forward with the divorce. Eddie continued walking all over me, as he did throughout our entire relationship. And there I was—still madly in love with him—praying that he would find his way back to me. That being said, I'm hardly a shrinking violet. We would get into some crazy-heated arguments that would, naturally, lead into some of the most intense and passionate sex of our relationship. I knew he was fucking another woman, but I couldn't help myself.

I was rarely insecure, but I would ask Eddie from time to time if my vagina was the same after childbirth, praying it was still tight enough for him. He always said yes, except once—and that was the first step on my road to Dr. Matlock.

Eddie had started taking Propecia, like many men, because he was concerned about hair loss. He had fantastic hair, but who was I to sideline his vanity? I appreciated that he took care of himself, but this particular drug has a lot of nasty side effects—including ones that happened in the bedroom. I knew he was concerned about his hairline, but momma needed something hard. I was not down for a limp dick and gave him an ultimatum: it was the Propecia or me.

Eddie never took well to being cornered . . . or criticized. So it was no surprise that he immediately shot back that my lady business wasn't what it used to be, either. He was actually quite vulgar and said something I don't care to repeat, so pardon my momentary filter. Please enjoy this moment. It doesn't happen often.

I could tell he immediately regretted saying it, but the damage was done. I already had my insecurities after having two children. I always kept myself together, working out and eating well, because our marriage and our sex life were important to me. But when it comes to a vagina, there's not much you can do beyond surgery. It wasn't necessarily a hot dog in a hallway, but it had definitely changed. Pushing out two babies will do that.

I remember in detail the last time we made love. He was living in the guest room at the time and we had gotten into yet another knock-down, drag-out fight, and, as always, instead of dealing with it, he headed toward the door.

This was a particularly bad fight, so it didn't surprise me when he disappeared for a few days, leaving me alone with the boys. It was a picturesque afternoon in Calabasas, and I was sitting in the backyard watching Mason and Jake take turns on the waterslide. Our backyard was like a beautiful playground, something we could never have afforded if we lived on the other side of the hill (translation: Beverly Hills). I was enjoying the sunshine in one of the few peaceful moments I had those days when my phone rang. It was a gossip reporter asking me for my reaction. "My reaction to what?" I asked. Apparently, while I sat at home with our children the night before, my husband was attending a Kings of Leon concert at the Hollywood Bowl with his girl-friend.

"Wow," I thought. "He isn't even trying to hide it anymore." I called the nanny outside to keep an eye on the boys while I went inside to go rifle through his room. Of course it was an invasion of his privacy, but I didn't give a fuck. When I tried to turn the knob, I discovered a lock was on the door. We never had locks in our house (except for the outside of Jakey's kiddie corral, but I already explained my decision for that). I felt my blood begin to boil. I grabbed the phone and started calling his cell phone over and over. Of course, he didn't pick up, but I'm certain he knew I had figured it out.

I spent the rest of the day working myself into a frenzy, so when he finally returned home that night, I went for the jugular. I was screaming at the top of lungs, "How could you do this? How could you go out in public with her?" He didn't say a word and headed for his room. When he finally managed to unlock the door, with me screaming over his shoulder, I tried to bulldoze my way into his room. He turned around and tried pushing me back out the door. Somewhere between the yelling and the pushing and the tears, we started kissing. Not an apology kiss or an I-love-you kiss, but an angry kiss. It was a go-fuck-yourself kiss. But we didn't fuck ourselves; we fucked each other. Hate sex, it turns out, is pretty hot, but I knew then that I didn't want that. Not with Eddie. Not anymore. When it was over and we were lying on the floor of the guest room—the room I apparently was no longer allowed access to, despite being in my home—I felt bruised and broken. In that moment, I knew I never wanted to feel that way again. This would be the last time Eddie ever touched me.

And I knew only one way that I would for certain keep this promise to myself. I was about to be reborn—or, rather, rejuvenated.

I was at the nail salon flipping through one of the glossy fashion magazines when I came across this piece called "The Secret Plastic Surgery No One Wants to Talk About." I was intrigued. The article discussed in detail the rising trend of vaginal-rejuvenation surgery. When

I got home, I started doing some research on the procedure. (Surfing the Internet became my new hobby. See Chapter 7. #GossipSlut) and discovered that it was basically the equivalent of a tummy tuck for the inside of your kitty cat. There was usually the exterior, add-on option of the labia-lift, but that would most likely cost extra and eww. As for me, I've always subscribed to the school of thought that men don't really care what it looks like—pink, gray, hair, no hair, landing strip—to them, it's all the same. Once they get to that point, they're not going to turn back because you never got laser hair removal on your lady business. I looked for local doctors who performed this surgery and stumbled on Dr. Matlock, one of the pioneers in modern vagino-plasty. I immediately decided to schedule a consultation and thought it was best if I went by myself. I was a little embarrassed at first and never thought I would ever be sharing it (especially in a book!), so I first wanted to navigate these waters by myself, to see if it was something I could actually see myself doing.

When I arrived at Dr. Matlock's Beverly Hills office, I could tell that a couple of the nurses were clearly up-to-date on their celebrity gossip and recognized me right away. But they couldn't have been any sweeter. I filled out all the paperwork, still not sure if this was for me, but I wanted to hear what the doctor had to say. Dr. Matlock immediately made me feel at ease in what could have been an uncomfortable situation. He informed me that, despite my concerns, I was in great shape for a thirty-six-year-old mother of two and a rejuvenation wasn't necessary; however, if it was something I really wanted, he could definitely help me with a kitty-cat upgrade. I told him that I would read all the literature and take a few days to think about it. After all, this pretty intense surgery had an even more intense price tag: $12,000. Plus, the recovery period was at least two weeks, and I would need someone on hand to take care of me. The boys had the nanny, but I couldn't exactly ask her to help me with a catheter. I mean, I could, but I'm pretty sure she would have charged me extra.

I had already undergone some fairly painful LEEPs for the HPV I'd contracted, so was I really going to put myself through this because of him, too?

Later that night, over a glass of sauvignon blanc, it occurred to me: a brand-new vagina would be an Eddie-free vagina. It would be something completely unknown to him and would offer me the fresh start I so desperately deserved. It was time for my pussy to be reborn. I understand that, to many of you, this may seem like an extreme measure to take to cut someone out of your life. But I've always been an extreme kind of girl, with extreme emotions. I loved this man so much and so hard that I needed a reason to never let him touch me again.

I called to schedule the surgery, and when the nurse asked how I was going to pay for the procedure, I decided that since Eddie had ruined my vagina for me, he could pay for a new one. I gave her Eddie's credit-card number—the same one he'd canceled for a brief period after reading a negative quote about him I gave to the press.

The next step was to get Eddie out of the house. Not only was it completely unhealthy for us to be living under the same roof, but I also didn't need him hanging around and asking questions while I recovered. For a while, I tolerated his living there because it was a way to hold on to him and to hope that we could one day be fixed. But after making love to him through tears and anger, I realized he was a perfect stranger to me now. How could I want something back that never existed? I couldn't unknow everything I had discovered, and I didn't want to. I liked the woman I was becoming—slowly, but surely—and I was interested in where this new road would take me.

So I got Eddie out of the house the quickest way I knew how: I called my mom. Once I informed him that my mother was coming to stay for two weeks, Eddie immediately got an apartment at the Oakwood in Woodland Hills—the land of furnished housing for temporary residents and cheating spouses. I didn't tell my mom why I needed her to come stay until after she had already touched down at LAX. I was still a bit embarrassed about going through with the procedure, but I was also convinced she would always be supportive no matter how insane I sounded or what I decided to do with my body. She's my mom. She thinks I'm perfect just as I am, but I also knew she wouldn't be judgmental about the procedure.

I was nervous leading up to the procedure, and I was on so many medications afterward that my memory of that time is a little foggy. I've enlisted my mother, Judy Glanville, to offer her recollection, as well:

It was August 2009 when Brandi called to ask if I could make a trip down to LA. She told me that she needed me to stay for two weeks because she was going to have a surgical procedure that was going to require bed rest. At first, I figured it had something to do with her interstitial cystitis (chronic bladder inflammation) and that she needed some help caring for the boys, as well as herself.

Brandi picked me up at the airport. When we arrived at the house, Eddie had still not fully moved out, although he was noticeably absent during my visit. The children were told their dad was staying in the other bedroom, because he was snoring too much for Mommy. They were so young and still unaware of what was going on.

Brandi handed me some papers and said she needed me to read them. The papers consisted of pre- and postoperative instructions for patients undergoing vaginal-rejuvenation laser surgery, as well as what the surgery entailed, and I committed them to memory as best I could. (Brandi's note: My mom could not have been more supportive. When I finally mustered up the courage to tell her what I was about to do, she lifted up her hand to give me a high five. She said, "Brandi, you are such a strong girl. I support whatever you need to do to get over this asshole and out of this mess." She never ceases to amaze me.)

The day of the surgery, Eddie's father, Carl, picked Brandi and me up and drove us to the surgery center in Beverly Hills. The doctor's office had mistakenly told Brandi the wrong time, so if her nerves weren't already going crazy, now she had more time to wait and think about it. Carl and I stayed with Brandi for a while, until she told us to go out and grab lunch. Then Brandi texted me that she was going in, so Carl and I went for a walk. We kept our conversations out of Eddie and Brandi's private business, because that was going to get us nowhere. When he and I returned to the center, we waited . . . and waited. It felt like forever.

By the time Brandi was alert enough to go home, it was already dark outside. Carl started the forty-five-minute journey back to Calabasas, but had a hard time seeing at night. Brandi was on the verge of a panic attack, so I decided it was better if he pulled over and I drove us the rest of the way—we didn't need to get into an accident hours after the surgery.

When we got back to the house—safe and sound—Carl and I immediately put Brandi to bed. She had a urinary catheter in her bladder, which was to stay in for several days, so she would not have to get up to use the bathroom, but more important, to keep the vaginal and perineal area clean. That first evening, Brandi was still numb from the local anesthesia they had injected into the surgical site, but it didn't last long.

The next morning, she was in so much pain that we called the office to have a nurse come to the house to administer more anesthesia injections. (Brandi's note: If you do choose this surgery and, like me, need a house call from a nurse, just know that it's insanely expensive. I sort of wish I'd just toughed it out.) *When that wore off, Brandi was again in so much pain that we called the clinic. This time they told us to come back to the center.*

It was dark, and I was forced to drive despite being completely unfamiliar with Los Angeles. Brandi was in agony, clearly not in the happiest of moods, but she had to help me with directions back to Beverly Hills (most of which were delivered in a loud, irritated voice). When we got there, she went immediately into the doctor's room, but, yet again, whatever they gave her wore off a few hours after we got back home.

Brandi's nerves were now raw, and she was in excruciating pain. She said she felt as if the balloon of saline solution that keeps the catheter in the bladder had shifted and that the catheter had pulled out of the bladder and gone into the urethra.

I had experience dealing with catheters when I was a nurse's aide earlier in my life, so I decided to deflate the balloon and remove the catheter myself. When I called the clinic to tell them what had happened, they told us it was essential that the catheter remain in place, so off we went again . . . back to Beverly Hills. Since nothing else seemed to work, the doctor gave Brandi a prescription for pain medication and told her to routinely apply ice packs to the perineum. The medication caused some additional minor complications, which caused even more discomfort, but we endured.

The boys were home during all of this, but were being cared for by the nanny and Eddie's parents. I also chipped in whenever Brandi was resting. As part of my job, I was to keep the children from bounding into the bedroom and onto the bed. They are both lovey, cuddly, snuggly boys who were used to lots of physical contact from Mom, so it was confusing for them not to be able to play with her and roughhouse with her. It was especially tough for Jake, who was only two years old at the time, with Mommy at the center of his little world.

They weren't thrilled that I wouldn't let them in the room, but I did earn some bonus points when we went swimming, because I would actually swim underwater and get my hair wet. (Mom would never *get her hair wet!) Besides that, I cooked a few meals (one of which was a sandwich for Brandi that she complained about, because she didn't approve of the bread. I knew the bread wasn't really a big deal and that it was just a way for her to blow off a little steam), played games, and watched a lot of* Max and Ruby.

Seven days after the surgery, Brandi was already up and moving. I was packing up and getting ready to head back to Sacramento when my cell phone started ringing. The number on the caller ID said it was a reporter from People *magazine. I decided it was best not to answer, but I immediately told Brandi. She asked me for my cell phone and went out back to take the call.* (Brandi's note: The reporter had called to ask about rumors that Eddie was house-hunting with LeAnn. After hearing the entire story, I declined to comment. I didn't know anything, anyway. I had been busy the last few days.) *As I watched Brandi walk around the yard on the cell phone, she saw a baby rattlesnake come down the waterslide and into their pool. Without so much as a flinch, she got the pool skimmer and pulled the snake out of the water—while still on the phone. Snakes had always terrified her, so I was in awe of her newfound courage. She calmly walked the net over to the back fence and tossed the little guy back into the wilderness. I remember thinking how proud I was of her. My daughter was such a good person.*

It was a painful time, both emotionally and physically, for Brandi, and emotionally for me. I wanted so badly to be able to fix everything, but that was not within the realm of possibility. So I tried to be there for her the best way I knew how, helping her take care of her new "kitty cat."

* * *

While I don't remember much, I do remember that the recovery period was beyond what I'd imagined it would be. It was more painful than childbirth. It was absolute hell. My boob job didn't hurt at all and everyone had told me it would, so I figured it would be the same for vaginal rejuvenation. Not true. I felt as if I were on fire and I could do nothing to make it stop. I wanted desperately to crawl out of my own skin. My muscles were totally clenched at all times, and I couldn't imagine a worse pain. I thought in the back of my head that maybe God was punishing me or trying to teach me some medieval lesson. Perhaps I'd let my ego get the best of me, and I was now paying the price. I remember thinking, "Hell must be an eternal recovery period from vaginal rejuvenation." I was so clouded that the days blurred together. I was certain something was wrong, that I would never be back to normal, that I shouldn't have gone through with this stupid fucking procedure, and then, finally, "Oh my God, I'm dying." The silver lining was that in those few days of extreme pain, I didn't think once about Eddie or what's-her-face. It sounds bizarre, but I sort of understood why some people would cause physical harm to themselves when going through emotionally difficult times. Physical pain can make you forget just about everything else.

Since I'm allergic to hydrocodone—the main ingredient in Vicodin—they gave me Percocet when I went back that third time with my mother. During the procedure, the doctor used a laser instrument to cut the inside of my vaginal wall and sewed me up using dissolvable stitches. Afterward, I was told absolutely nothing was to go inside my vagina for six weeks—no tampons, no cock, no vibrators, and no fingers (I wish my mom were in the room for that conversation). It was just like after childbirth; nothing was to enter my kitty cat for a month and a half then, so I already knew I could do it.

I was bedridden for roughly a week and should have stayed longer, but my mommy duties called. The boys would no longer stand for an inactive mommy, so I needed to get a move on. Plus, I get bored easily. I'm grateful, however, that I had that week. I wouldn't have been able to go through the surgery—something I knew I needed to cleanse myself of Eddie—if I hadn't had Mommy to come stay with me.

No matter how old you are, there's no cozier feeling than to have your mom take care of you. After I had Mason, my mom stayed with me for an entire month. He was her first grandchild, and she is absolutely amazing with babies. (I think it's a gift you acquire after having and raising three children of your own.) She was by my side for a week and a half after Jakey was born, but already had four grandchildren by the time Jake arrived . . . and had to race back up north for the birth of number five. Busy Grandma.

Once the pain had subsided, I felt absolutely new again. I felt as if I had rid myself of any last vestige of Eddie. But most important, it gave me a fresh outlook on my future—a future that was beginning to look brighter and tighter. I anticipated being totally blown away by the results. I should have been for $12,000, right?

Truthfully, though, I wasn't sure if it even worked properly! I mean, how would I be able to tell until I actually used it? So, my hunt began for the perfect man to give up my "second virginity" to. While I was eager to get back on the horse (so to speak), I was going to be exceptionally picky. I had this budding new flower, and the recipient was in for a special treat. The only thing I was sure of was it wasn't going to be Eddie.

Well, it didn't take long for Eddie to call about the bill. A week after the surgery, he was on the phone screaming, "What the fuck cost you twelve thousand dollars? Who the fuck is Dr. Matlock? Did you get a nose job?"

I responded simply, "Yes. A nose job." And I hung up the phone. My phone rang again about five minutes later: Eddie. This time I didn't answer. It rang again—and then again. "Ahh," I thought. Eddie must have discovered Dr. Matlock on Google. I decided it was probably best to avoid his calls for the next few days while he cooled off.

Even though Carl drove me to the surgery (he thought I was totally crazy, but stayed with me anyway), and Eddie's mother knew exactly what was going on, they kept Eddie in the dark. At the time, they still considered me a daughter, so they let him figure it out on his own. It would only be a matter of time.

When we finally spoke a few days later, Eddie was still absolutely livid—partly because of the staggering price tag and partly because of his overwhelming jealousy that some other man would reap the benefits of his ex-wife's brand-new pussy. In hindsight, I know I shouldn't have put it on Eddie's card. I was being vengeful and it came back to bite me, because this was something I was hoping to keep private. And in what world would Eddie not immediately run to tell his new girlfriend? Naturally, this woman was beyond ecstatic to be in possession of this crazy personal information about me and started spreading it around like wildfire. It didn't take long for her minions to begin shouting my private business from the social-media rooftops. I, of course, denied it at first. I never thought it would be something I would open up about, but I also realized that it's nothing to be ashamed of, either.

It took me a long time to test my kitty cat out. I have to say that so far the reviews are stupendous, and I'm happy with the sensation myself. Eddie knows that he has never touched the "new" me, and that gives me so much joy. Now, every time I bend over at soccer practice and feel his eyes on my ass (yes, he still checks out my ass), I think, "You'll never touch me again . . . "

At the end of the day, we need to do whatever it takes to move on. Don't be ashamed of any decision you make, and stay strong. Much like the pain of recovering from vaginal rejuvenation, this, too, shall pass.

brandi's **babble**

Ultimately, my husband got a new vagina . . . and so did I.

CHAPTER **SEVEN**

Drinking and Tweeting

Remember the good old days when social media didn't exist? When the first thing you grabbed in the morning was a cup of coffee and not your iPhone and when personal privacy wasn't just a setting you have to select? I think of those pretech days as the golden years, when everything you said and did wasn't an opportunity to alert five hundred of your "closest" friends (and something that could come back and bite you in the ass later).

Social media has completely changed the way we interact with one another. Instead of calling your best friend for a movie night, now you send him or her a Facebook message. Instead of mailing baby announcements when you have a child, you blast it out on Instagram. And instead of your casual one-night Vegas wedding to your former friend's ex-husband one New Year's Eve's remaining between you, him, and the county clerk, it gets blasted to the Twitter-verse and ends up #Trending on every gossip site from here to Timbuktu. Oh, wait, that's just me. Either way, social media has made even the most intimate events something you share with not only everyone you've ever met, but complete strangers—narcissism at its finest. It's how people announce engagements, travel plans, weddings, pregnancies, new jobs, new relationships, new shoes, deaths, divorces, promotions, and even breakups.

I think social media is the enemy of anyone going through a split. Technology is no longer just how we connect with each other, it's how we disconnect with each other. You used to be able to break up with someone (a boyfriend, girlfriend, husband, wife, or friend), and he or she virtually disappeared from your life. And that's the way it's supposed to be, isn't it?

Sure, occasionally a certain sappy song or romantic movie would come on, and you'd wonder what he or she was up to, but there was no way to know. Of course, you could always pick up the phone (and more recently, text or e-mail), but that would require that person's knowing you were thinking of him or her. Where's the fun in that? You never want them to know you're thinking of them, so you refrain. Before long the memories start to fade. One day, you realize you can't quite remember how she smelled or the exact color of his eyes. Eventually, without ever knowing it, you just forget that person altogether. You replace old memories with new ones, and life goes on. It was the clean break you needed to move forward.

Well, Facebook fucked that up, didn't it? Welcome to 2013, ladies and gays. A breakup is no longer grabbing a tub of ice cream, a box of Kleenex, and watching *The Notebook*. Today, it's the chance to enter into a second, extremely unhealthy phase of your breakup: cyber-stalking. You know what I'm talking about. It's that impulse to constantly refresh his Twitter feed to see if he has posted anything new. Or that urge to routinely check Instagram for new photos of that face that you should already have long forgotten. So thanks to some dorky dude from Harvard—and the virtual parade of social media that followed—we can subject ourselves to this cruel form of self-torture. I was cursed with a front-row seat into my ex-husband's brand-new life without me.

Via his new girlfriend's Twitter page, I was pretty much able to witness every moment of their lives—partially because I was obsessed with tracking him, and partially because she loved to fucking post shit to piss me off (and still does). #FML. I knew better. You know better. We all know better. But that doesn't mean we're going to stop. It's completely masochistic, but strangely satisfying. After months of waffling, you finally decide that you have mustered enough courage to "unfollow" that person on Twitter or "defriend" him or her on Facebook—a decision you will undoubtedly regret when you're psychotically driven to check whether his profile photo has changed or when you're obsessively counting how many tweets he posted in your absence (especially if he is "private"). #CrazyTown. However, that's better than the alternative when one day you go to check his profile and you've been defriended, or worse . . . BLOCKED. #Gut-Punch. Or perhaps you're like me and never "friend" or "follow" your ex and his or her new partner to begin with. Instead, you stalk their profiles through mutual friends, because you don't want to give them the satisfaction of knowing that you follow them.

In my opinion, social media can easily become this all-consuming obsession that drives you to other vices (such as countless bottles of white wine).

However, I'm not entirely sure if I subscribe to the idea of "twee-hab" (in which people seek professional help for social-media addictions). I can totally relate to those people who feel social media has taken over their lives, but cyber-rehab? Really? If you have the kind of money to check yourself into therapy because you can't stop tweeting, go buy a fucking plane ticket to Maui and take a vacation instead.

For those people with preexisting dependencies and addictive personalities, it can be especially dangerous. And if that's the case, seeking medical treatment to help conquer those demons is commendable. I just don't believe that regular people need treatment just because they can't stop refreshing their news feeds.

But if you're like me, and you used social media as an emotional crutch to maintain some kind of self-destructive connection with someone that you should already have let go of, you don't need cyber-rehab, you need to take your life back. But like all things, it's easier discussed than done (except sex, which is easier done than discussed!).

I blame Eddie for breaking my heart, but I blame social media for keeping it broken for so long.

First of all, I'm completely technologically challenged. When I was growing up, my hippie-dippie family never had any fancy electronics—I don't think we even owned an electric can opener. My dad was much more concerned with his pot garden than he was with investing in a cassette player, plus his eight-tracks were just fine by him. We were the absolute last family on the planet to have a VCR or even an answering machine. And call-waiting? Forget it. To this day, my parents have zero idea how to check voice mail and are just learning how to send a text, which is difficult for my dad, who has three fingers on his left hand and no thumb. Recently, my sister attempted to set my dad up with a Facebook account, but when he inadvertently started giving interviews to his new "friends" (read: reporters), he decided take a break from social media. It's probably for the best.

Technology has never come easy for me (and things usually "come" very easy for me, haha). When my San Francisco modeling agent forced me to get a pager to contact me about casting alerts, I never figured out how to use the stupid thing. I missed a lot of castings. While I was overseas, cell phones weren't mainstream yet, so we got phone cards to use at random pay phones. I never figured out how to use them, so I would go months at a time without talking to anyone back home. We would actually—gasp!—write postcards. #OldenDays.

Then I met Eddie. In the thirteen-plus years we were together, he never wanted me near a computer. (Hmm, I wonder why?) Most women would find that completely controlling and manipulative, but I was totally fine with it. I've said it before, but I had no problem being a kept woman, and at the time I liked having my man tell me what to do. It was hot. Plus, any sort of technology terrified me—and still sort of does. Even my remote control freaks me out. (I have to ask my nine-year-old to record things for me.)

I was perfectly content living in the dark ages when we were together. Everything I thought I ever wanted was right in front of me, so what did I need a computer for? If I wanted my gossip, I would buy a magazine. If I wanted to shop, I would drive into Beverly Hills and hit up Rodeo Drive. If I wanted to talk to my friends or family, I would call them. If my parents wanted photos of the boys, I would have to mail them anyway. So, what was the point of figuring out the Internet?

Not until after I found out about the affair did I actually get behind a computer. I knew that if I was going to keep tabs on my husband (at the time, we were still trying to work things out), I had to get cyber-savvy. I wasn't going to be a sitting duck. If my husband was stepping out on me, I wanted to be able to go see the fucking photos on *PerezHilton* myself (instead of having a friend describe them to me over the phone) or watch the video of him kissing another woman on *Us Weekly* on a fucking loop.

When I finally grew the balls to try to "surf the Web," it took a while for me to figure out how to even turn the damn computer on!

I didn't have too much success at first, so I just focused on the basics: Google. I could "google" my husband's name, or his new girlfriend's name, and there was just such a crazy amount of information out there. I would scroll through all the past stories online, purposefully reliving painful memories—not necessarily a healthy activity for someone trying to forgive and forget. For hours at a time, I would click through pages and pages of stories about "LeAnn Rimes and Eddie Cibrian." I would dissect every photo of this woman with my hyper-critical eye, wondering what the hell my husband saw in this country singer. I was just so fucking baffled.

When a few weeks later a story came out in *In Touch* magazine that my husband was having yet another affair (this time he was fucking a Hooters waitress), I was able to grab a glass of wine and head straight to the computer to see for myself. After a few simple mouse clicks—and a huge gulp of sauvignon blanc—I landed on a gossip blog only to discover that the lead story had photos of my husband and some fucking slut having a great fucking time on my motherfucking boat. (This was the catalyst for motorcycle-tire-slashing-gate.) As always, my immediate reaction was to get even. I wanted my husband to feel the same absolute rage that I felt after seeing him with another woman—twice! I wasn't ready to go fuck someone else, so I took it out on the motorcycle tires.

Not long after, Eddie was out of the house and shacking up with his mistress—the country-music singer, not the cocktail waitress. (It's hard to keep them straight!) I was still living relatively under the radar despite the occasional weekly magazine outburst, so I wanted to find some way to rub my "fabulous" life in both of their faces. Don't get it twisted, my life was far from fabulous. But they didn't need to know that. My options were limited, so I began toying with the idea of "accidentally on purpose" leaking half-naked photos of myself twirling around a stripper pole to a gossip website. I figured that nothing would drive Eddie crazier than the idea of other men ogling his soon-to-be ex-wife. During our marriage, *Playboy* magazine expressed interest in photographing me, and it interested me, but Eddie told me he would leave me if I ever did anything like that. I was for his eyes only. So I knew having naked photos of me floating around the Internet would drive him insane. Luckily, I had a great, levelheaded friend who talked me out of that monster mistake. I didn't need those online so that one day my kids would stumble upon them. Instead, I discovered a different solution. Enter Facebook. My friend set me up on the social-media site and was exceptionally patient in teaching me how to navigate the system: "add friends," "post to my wall," "status updates," etc. Of course I had heard of Facebook—I wasn't completely dense—but I never had any interest in actually creating an account. I would constantly tease my friends about having accounts, referring to it as "Fuckbook," since everyone was connecting with exes and hooking up. For me, everything I cared to know about was living under my roof; it felt like an unnecessary addition to my already crazy world. But my life was changing, so I had to change with it, and I dove headfirst into the social-media pool. (Take my advice, dip your toes in first. It's a much better transition.)

Initially, my page was simply a platform for me to brag on. I wasn't "friends" with Eddie or LeAnn, but I knew that any information I shared online would eventually make its way to them via "friend" crossover. So, like any levelheaded, scorned ex-wife, I started posting trampy, drunk photos of my gorgeous girlfriends and me dancing in Barbie-doll-size dresses at Las Vegas nightclubs or lounging on tropical beaches wearing barely-there bikinis. I was desperate to send my notoriously jealous ex-husband into a green-with-envy tailspin after seeing how much fun I was having being single. And I wanted that country-music-singer girlfriend of his, whose only friends were on her payroll, to see how many wonderful people I had in my life—all despite my shattered marriage. I have to admit, I put up a fantastic front. To anyone looking, I was having the time of my life and going completely hog wild. In reality, I was going off the fucking tracks and was sad as hell.

At first, Facebook served merely as an opportunity to piss Eddie off, but after a while, I realized the other benefits of posting slutty photos of myself online: boys. My message box began filling up with flirty notes from all kinds of gorgeous men (and some not-so-attractive ones, too): friends of friends, former flings, and other blasts from the past. Facebook became more than just a passive-aggressive attempt to piss off Eddie, it became a chance to cyber-flirt with hot-ass, semifamous actors—and perhaps one or two of Eddie's former costars—to grab drinks with, go to dinner with, and, eventually, fuck the shit out of, to prove to myself that I was still desirable. For a while, I felt I had the upper hand. I could simultaneously piss off Eddie and find new guys to distract me. I was hooked. Facebook was my life.

Then, Twitter happened.

Twitter and I have a love-hate relationship. It's like an abusive boyfriend I keep going back to. I call it Battered Social-Media Syndrome. Twitter makes me feel terrible; Twitter makes me feel wonderful. Twitter supports me when I'm feeling depressed and beats me down when I'm feeling happy. I get into fights with Twitter and try to break up with it, but then I get lonely or have a few too many glasses of wine and go crawling back to it, with my tail between my legs.

Okay, if I thought Facebook was difficult to understand, Twitter felt fucking impossible. Like, what the fuck is a "hashtag"? How the hell do I "retweet"? I still haven't totally mastered the Twitter-verse, and it took me more than two years to get this far, but I did discover pretty quickly how to find LeAnn's Twitter page. She just couldn't keep her mouth shut and felt this incessant need to share every single moment of her life—with my family—with all of her Twitter followers. Checking her feed became my daily obsession. With Facebook, I had power. With Twitter, I was completely helpless.

Through her posts and photos, I was able to watch their adulterous love story unfold. Before long, she brought out the big guns: my kids. I could actually see these family photos of the woman who stole my husband sharing Christmas Eve dinner with my children, while I was home alone for my first Christmas without them.

I had this perverse window into their seemingly perfect little world: beach vacations, private jets, and family-photo shoots. These were my children. I gave birth to these two little boys and now have an insanely expensive vagina to prove it. Why did she get to be their mom, too? How was this fair? She got my husband. She took my kids. She stole my life. And she knew I was watching, and she was fucking ruthless. Everyone told me to stop looking, that I was self-sabotaging, but it became my addiction.

People who say that they don't check their exes' Facebook posts, Twitter pages, Instagram feeds, or Foursquare check-ins are completely full of shit. Every time that see-you-next-Tuesday would post some nurturing, cuddling photo with my children, I headed straight to the sauvignon blanc. #WineTherapy. I'm not even sure why I wasted a clean glass, because I knew I was downing that entire bottle. It was like cyber-cutting. I had to see what she was doing. I had to know where my boys were (since I still didn't have a fucking cell phone number for either of them or a house line). It was my only glimpse into their world. To this day, if I can't get ahold of my boys, I will check her Twitter, and nine times out of ten, I can figure out exactly where they are. Oh, no wonder my son isn't answering our FaceTime call, he's having a great time playing in the ocean . . . in fucking Mexico! I try to step away, but as the saying goes, curiosity killed the cat—or, in my case, the cougar.

There is a huge part of me that wishes I couldn't check

in on them. It never stops hurting. It gets easier, but it's still a little painful. I can only imagine the strange sense of relief I would feel if I woke up tomorrow and I couldn't google my husband's name or cyber-stalk his wife's Twitter page. But there's no use living in Fantasyland. (I did that for thirteen years, and look how it turned out.)

My only regret now is that I didn't hop on the technology bandwagon sooner. I would have forced my husband to get a smartphone so it would have been easier to keep tabs on his cheating ass. It would have been a little bit more difficult for him to lie about where he was sleeping, if I forced him to make a FaceTime call to me before bed. (But beware, no one looks good on FaceTime. For being so advanced, couldn't Apple have cooked up a better camera solution?) And maybe if I could have tracked his whereabouts with some fucking iPhone app and known that he wasn't playing golf, but having dinner with his married girlfriend in Laguna Beach . . . Knowing that I had this intelligence, he would have stayed on his best behavior—and perhaps I'd still be married today. The downside being that I'd still be married to Eddie Cibrian.

* * *

Not only has technology changed the way we break up, it's transformed how we date altogether. Social media and the Internet have all but completely eliminated the concept of the blind date. If your friend sets you up with a fiftysomething real estate developer, all you have to do is google his name to find out almost anything about him—where he works, where he lives, what he looks like.

Once you actually start dating someone new, there's an entirely new set of cyber rules by which to play. Before, you knew you were in a committed relationship after a conversation and a piece of jewelry or, for our parents, a letterman jacket. Today, it's changing your Facebook status to "in a relationship" and your profile picture to some Instagram-filtered shot of the two of you. If you're really seeking some attention (which, let's face it, we all are or else we would delete these stupid accounts), you change your status to "it's complicated" whenever you're having a fight—or when you're separated but still legally married. Nothing perks up someone's interest more than coming across an "it's complicated" status. When you break up, as most people do these days, it becomes a story for all of your "friends" to see on the Facebook news feed.

I still pretty much hate all technology and the entire concept of social media (except when I'm loving it); however,
I'm pretty sure it's here to stay. Don't get me wrong, I'm a
total #TwitterWhore and I google just about everything and
everyone, but I also recognize how, at times, it has taken
over my life. Just ask yourself how many times you have
interrupted a wonderful night with friends and family to
post on Facebook or Twitter that you're having a wonderful night. How many times have you stopped midsentence
to ask a waiter to take a photo and then spent the next five
minutes fucking with filters to post it on Instagram? It's as
if we have this strange obsession with proving to the world
that we are, in fact, cool. Look, I'm totally guilty of this, and
I'm not sure I ever intend to stop. It's just the culture we live
in now, but it's important to keep things in perspective.

With any new advancement comes its pitfalls. For every
positive, there must be a negative. Good doesn't exist without
evil. You know, like yin and yang and all that Zen crap?

To me, one of the biggest downfalls of this new age
of technology is the emergence of cyber-bullying. Let
me say first and foremost that cyber-bullying does exist.
Take the twelve-year-old girl in Chicago, Illinois, whose
classmates created a Facebook page dedicated solely

to making nasty comments about her weight and was forced to face her victimizers every day. Or the gay college student whose roommate posted an explicit personal video of him on YouTube and who decided to take his own life rather than tell his family and friends that he was a homosexual. Those are real, serious, and tragic accounts of cyber-bullying.

However, I do think this culture is way too liberal with its definition of cyber-bullying. If, hypothetically, you're a country-music singer and public figure who decides to engage with one of the millions of "haters" online—whom you never have to actually see—that is not cyber-bullying. If you can close your computer or turn off an app without the repercussions of actually having to deal with these people in your real life and not your cyber life, it's not fucking bullying. If you decided, hypothetically, to contact a mutual Twitter follower to get this hater's phone number and call him or her, that person is not cyber-bullying you. I've experienced my fair share of actual bullying in my life, but I have not been cyber-bullied. Sure, I've had people who, let's say, work for a certain blond former Nashville resident send nasty, mean, and cruel messages to me on Facebook and Twitter. I've had people call me ugly names and make horrible accusations about my life, but that is not bullying. I don't have to go to work every day and be harassed by these people. I'm not forced to interact with them on the playground. At any time, I can close the fucking window and walk away.

When you choose to open up your life via social media and allow random people to interact with you, you can't get upset if someone in Middle America wants to call you fat, ugly, or, perhaps, a homewrecker.

I've learned firsthand that when you're a public figure (even someone as minor as a reality personality), everybody has an opinion. It's easy to spit insults from an anonymous account while sitting in your basement in Anywhere, USA, so I never take what people say to heart. Miserable people love to make other people miserable. I don't hate those people, I just feel sorry for them.

My philosophy is that if you have the balls to post a negative comment online, you better be prepared to say it to that person's face—and if you're a big enough pussy to create a fake account to publicly criticize someone, you really should find a hobby. I've never been one to mince words, so if I decide to post something negative online, I would have no problem saying it to that person's face. If

I post that someone was being a bitch today, odds are I've already told that person that she was being a fucking bitch today. Occasionally, I have been known to have a few too many glasses of wine and start reacting to the more negative tweets. It's like today's equivalent of drunk dialing. Sometimes the wine starts flowing, and you just can't help telling the shitheads to go fuck themselves. I know, it's not a good idea, but you know what? #SueMe.

So, if you do choose to be an active member of the cyberworld, here are my rules for being a responsible social-media citizen:

1. Do not allow yourself to be victimized by shitty people. No one else should have control over how you feel about yourself.

2. I think Kenny Rogers said it best: you got to know when to fold 'em. If you are on the receiving end of offensive tweets, posts, or messages, turn off the computer and walk away.

3. Don't be a fucking hypocrite. People are all too eager to post negative comments about other people online but want to cry "cyber-bullying"

when they are on the receiving end of nasty comments. Boo-fucking-hoo. If you're going to dish it, you better be prepared to take it.

4. Don't ever make a fake account. That's just completely spineless and seriously lame.

5. If you decide to post a shitty comment online about someone, you should have the backbone to say it to his or her face.

6. Everybody has seen a sunset. Nobody wants to see a picture of the sunset you saw. And if you're lame enough to want to see someone else's photo of a sunset, guess what, go outside around 6:00 p.m. and watch the sun motherfucking set.

7. Girls and gays, be nice. If you post a photo where you look amazing and your friends look like shit, you're just a fucking dick—and a terrible friend.

8. If you're going to tweet it or post it, you better believe it. If it's not something you will be comfortable with existing online forever,

don't fucking put it up. And don't ever delete it, because by doing so, you're admitting you did or said something wrong.

9. Know your social-media boundaries. If you're currently in a relationship, it's not okay to be tweeting or facebooking with anyone who has sucked your face or your privates.

10. And, above all, don't drink and tweet. #Hypocrite.

brandi's **babble**

Follow me @brandiglanville. #TwitterWhore.

CHAPTER **EIGHT**

My Favorite Threesome

"Mom, do cheaters go to hell?"

I always assumed that my nine-year-old, Mason, had a pretty good idea of what had happened between his daddy and me, but not until he got a little older did he start to ask questions. I saw the fear in my little boy's eyes that his daddy was damned for eternity for being unfaithful to his family. Okay, to be fair, I may have shouted at Eddie to "go to hell" more than a dozen times before it was all said and done, but never in front of the children. Despite everything Eddie had put me through, I always wanted to shield the boys from the mess that was whirling around us.

"Why would you ask that?" I responded.

Mason shrugged and looked back out the window of the car. "I just want to know if cheaters are bad."

"Cheater!" Jake shouted. I looked back in the rearview mirror and saw the smile spread across his dimpled face. I was grateful that at least for today, he was still too young to understand what was going on.

The parent rumor-mill talk must have trickled down to the children in Mason's class, and my heart sank thinking that my son was now subject to all the whispers I'd been battling for months. I know that when he is older, he will read about the entire ordeal on the Internet and see the now-infamous video, and perhaps when he's thirty years old, I'll actually let him read this book. But I wasn't yet prepared for the "Daddy cheated on Mommy" conversation.

On most mornings the boys spend with me, we hop in the car at 7:30 a.m. and head to the Valley for school. I knew Mason was already aware of what a cheater is, since we would always listen to KIIS FM on our drive. During the station's morning show (the most kid-friendly one in Los Angeles, I might add!), a segment titled "Ryan's Roses" is intended to catch people who are unfaithful in their relationship. In the bit, someone pretends to be a florist and calls the presumed cheater to ask him or her where he or she would like a free batch of a roses sent, while the person's partner (who assumes the person is cheating) is quietly on the line. Some kind of on-air confrontation occurs, but if you're already unsure whether your partner would send his or her free dozen roses to you, it can't be that big of a surprise.

Mason looked at me expectantly, waiting for an answer.

"No, honey, they don't go to hell. They're not bad people, they're just not great husbands or wives."

I'm not sure if that was the right answer, but I didn't know what else to tell him. While I would never want my sons to grow up with resentment toward their father or to think he's a bad person, I also don't want them to grow up believing that infidelity is acceptable in any relationship. It was a fine line, and I was walking it the best I could. That being said, the idea of Mason's or Jake's ever dating someone special is such a foreign concept to me right now. Right now, they are *my* boys, and I will keep them that way as long as I can. I don't like to share.

I am lucky. I had two good reasons to get over my

divorce and move on with my life: Mason and Jake. While children aren't the only reason for living—many people suffer breakups with no kids involved—my children saved my life. If it weren't for those two little men, I would either be rocking a straitjacket in a padded room or be at the Betty Ford Center. I checked out of my life for a good while, and if it weren't for them, I don't think I would have had a reason to check back in. For a long time, Mason and Jake were the only reasons I would get out of bed in the morning, wash my face, and put one foot in front of the other. On plenty of days, I would rather have sat in bed all day watching sad movies and crying, but I was a mom and they needed me. So fighting the urge to crawl back under the covers and into my hole of self-pity, I would get up and go about my day. Many couples never have children, which makes a split that much cleaner—at least one would hope. I have come to enjoy the time I get to focus on my self-betterment when the boys are with their father, but during the transition, they were my two best reasons to move forward, and I'll always be grateful to them for that.

If you're going through a split without children, you have reason to be grateful for that, too. While my boys were a huge blessing when I was struggling with my divorce, and continue to be the light of my world, I have to deal with their father for the rest of my life. Breakups and divorces are much easier to move on from without children. You can wash your hands of your former part-ner, you'll never have to deal with that person again, and you definitely won't be ambushed by yet another paparazzi set-up at your kid's soccer game by his or her new partner. #JustSayin.

Look, when it comes to raising children after divorce, I don't have all the answers. I barely have any answers for raising children in general—especially in Los Angeles. When I was going through the thick of my divorce, friends recommended a thousand books and websites about how to tactfully explain to the boys what was going on and how to make the transition as easy as possible. However, mine was a unique situation. The shelves weren't neces-sarily brimming with books titled *What to Do When Your Husband Has an Affair with a Semi-Famous Country Singer*. It breaks my heart to think that my children will one day be able to relive every painful moment of this ugly ordeal, because it is forever cataloged on the Internet.

I decided not to tell the boys about Eddie's and my

separation—not immediately, anyway. How could I? I could barely accept it myself. At the time, part of me was still hoping that he would one day come home. I know ultimately it was my decision to end things. He kept telling me his affair was over, but I kept catching him in lies. He wouldn't shake this woman, and I simply could not trust him anymore. Despite all of that, I stalled in telling the boys the truth and instead kept telling them that Daddy was working. Daddy was always "working," so it wasn't anything new to them. I realized it was also a lie I often told myself when my husband would be on a trip for days on end and not call. I think taking your time in telling your kids is okay. You need to heal first before figuring out the right time and the right words. And Eddie's schedule was the perfect excuse.

Throughout both of my sons' lives, Eddie was always traveling for work—Romania, Morocco, Canada, New York, Washington, DC. It wouldn't seem out of the ordinary for him to be out of the house for lengthy periods. I decided early on that I would never say anything bad to the boys about their father. Every child deserves a father he or she can look up to and respect, even if it is Eddie Cibrian.

Mason finally figured out that Daddy wasn't coming

home when he moved out of the Oakwood apartments and into a rental home in the gated community of Mont Calabasas (only about a mile away from the home we'd shared). There, Eddie introduced the boys to his new friend, "Le," despite promising via his lawyers that he would refrain from bringing her around the boys until after the holidays and not until January 2010. Like most promises Eddie made, he wasn't prepared to keep this one, either. LeAnn had recently moved out of the Brentwood home she'd shared with her then husband, Dean, and into a rental in Hidden Hills. A soon-to-be-divorced, childless woman was consciously deciding to move from Brentwood to Calabasas? #SoPathetic.

"We met Le again," Mason told me one day over a bowl of cereal.

"Okay," I said. I had no other words and focused my attention back on unloading the dishwasher. I have always been extremely domestic, but since my divorce, I could no longer afford the help I was once accustomed to, so I was learning to do things on my own again.

"She sings songs that they play on the radio. Do you listen to her music?" Mason was testing me, studying my reaction, and I knew what was coming next.

"No, Mason, I don't." I didn't want to lie to him, but I didn't want to bash her, either. With Eddie's track record, I wasn't exactly sure how long she would be around; but for now, it appeared that she was going to be in the boys' lives for the foreseeable future, and they seemed to like her. Even though they were little, they are their own people, and I wanted them to develop their own opinion of her. Eventually, they will know the full story, and they can process that information however they like.

"Daddy kissed her," Mason said, looking directly at me. #GutPunch. He wanted to see if I would get sad. It wasn't manipulative; he was six years old at the time, and he was just trying to understand a confusing situation. I tried to muster some calm response, but I couldn't help the tears from welling up.

"Okay," I quickly managed, and darted out of the kitchen. I locked myself in the master bathroom for the next five minutes and allowed myself to sob. Of course Eddie and LeAnn kissed. I saw the video with my own eyes months earlier, and I know that kissing was just the tip of their sexual iceberg, regardless of how unattractive he always said he found her.

This was different. My children were watching their father be affectionate with a woman other than their mother. Not only was it strange for them, it was difficult for me, too.

Mason didn't say another word about it when I returned to the kitchen—sunglasses on—and we went about our day as normal. Later that night, after all the lights were out, Mason crawled into bed with me to snuggle. I think part of him felt that it was his job to take care of me now. And I let him. Every night he spent at my house for the next two years, Mason would crawl into bed to cuddle with me. Once Mason got a little too old to crawl into bed with Mommy, Jake took over cuddle duty. To this day, Jake still crawls into bed with me during the night, and I like it that way. Their cuddles helped because it showed how much they care about me. I knew they were going to be good men. Despite it all, I was raising good men.

Jake first realized that our life was changing when he waddled into Eddie's closet and found it completely empty. He was so confused and wondered where all of Daddy's clothes went. I had two giant walk-in closets in our Calabasas house (each one the size of my entire bedroom in my Encino rental), so I took half of the clothes I didn't wear and moved them over to Eddie's closet, thinking this would distract Jake for a while. The next day, he peeked into Eddie's closet and screamed, "No! No pink dresses in Daddy's closet." He burst into tears, so I scooped him up, held him tight, and started crying, too. I tried my best not to cry in front of the boys. For a few months I commonly wore sunglasses in the house, so they wouldn't see my puffy eyes. I wanted to be a strong mom that they could be proud of, but every so often my emotions would get the best of me.

Shortly after the kissing conversation, I finally admitted to the boys that Daddy wasn't coming home. LeAnn was now a frequent figure at his house, and I wasn't sure what they were learning about our situation over there, since Eddie and I weren't communicating. I decided that they might as well hear the truth from their mom, before they heard it elsewhere.

Finally, I just sucked it up and blurted out, "Daddy fell in love with someone else, and he's not going to live with us anymore." It shattered my heart to tell them that, but it was as close to the truth as I could get. I knew that as they got older, they would hear the story, but I would protect them as long as I could. Plus, I was pretty certain LeAnn and Eddie weren't coughing up the truth on their end. By this point, the boys were already used to the split living situation: two bedrooms, two closets, and two families. "The conversation" didn't seem to faze them too much, but as a parent, I found it a therapeutic discussion for us to have. I felt as if a weight had been lifted off my shoulders, since I had been keeping this massive secret from the two most important people in my life. It was providing a sense of closure to our former family. Many doors were still open, but as they say, one day at a time.

Mason had known what was going on for a while, but Jake seemed to finally understand as well. Now almost six years old, Jakey has zero recollection of the time Mommy and Daddy were married. Not too long ago, he picked up one of the photos I have displayed in my office from my friend Emma and Bruce Willis's wedding. The group shot of all of us shows Eddie and me smiling in the back row on what would prove to be our final vacation together, and I could see the confusion creep onto Jake's face. "You and Daddy were together here," he said, with a squinty nose and pointing his chubby, little finger at the frame.

"Yes," I told him. "We used to be husband and wife."

He looked back at the photo and started to giggle. "Weird," he said, before placing the picture back down. While part of me feels sad that he'll never remember the days when we were a happy family, the other part of me feels that he's lucky not to remember. Perhaps that will make it easier for him down the road.

Shortly after the holidays, Eddie moved out of his rental and into a gorgeous Hidden Hills home with his girlfriend, seven months after we separated. Of course, Eddie jumped at the opportunity to move in with her; he always wanted to move to that ultraluxurious gated community. Now that he had a sugar mama to pay the rent, why not upgrade his house? (Today, they're still living in their high-end rental, but have been spotted shopping for multimillion-dollar properties within the ritzy community. I guess LeAnn doesn't have any dreams of heading back to Nashville. #TooBad)

When he moved into his new rental with LeAnn, I was certain an engagement was on the horizon. He'd promised me over and over that he would never marry

LeAnn, but that was just one of the countless lies he told me. Soon, LeAnn Rimes would become my sons' bonus mom.

As soon as Eddie introduced her into the boys' world, she immediately began showering them with over-the-top gifts. She was trying to buy my kids' love, instead of earning it, and I felt the overwhelming need to compete. When the boys got home from yet another decadent vacation during which "Le" got them this and "Le" got them that, I decided I wanted to be the favorite for a while. I took Mason and Jake to Disneyland and splurged on an exclusive $700 tour guide for what I was calling our "special day." I'm also terrible at directions, so the guide came in handy. We had such a great day, and for a little while I was the best mom in the boys' world. I guess I shouldn't have been surprised when later that same week LeAnn and Eddie took the boys back to Disneyland. Couldn't they even let me have fucking Disneyland? When I saw the boys a few days later, all they could talk about was how much more fun they had with Daddy and "Le," because they didn't have to wait in any lines. I guess when you've sung a couple country songs, they don't make you wait in line at Disneyland any-more.

Let's get real: the boys have always been spoiled. Both Eddie and I grew up with virtually nothing. We came from modest upbringings—hell, we lived in ghettos. I lived somewhere between the Bloods and the Crips, who all nicknamed me Barbie. Eddie grew up in a similar neighborhood deep in the Valley. (His parents had come over from Cuba.) When we had the boys, we wanted to give them everything: the fancy house, a big pool, and the extravagant toys. We thought, "We're going to have these great kids who have everything." It didn't take long for us to realize that we were spoiling them rotten. To raise decent children, especially those close to all the bullshit of Hollywood, we needed to teach them the right life lessons. I wanted them to learn the value of a dollar. I may have gone overboard and scarred them a bit, because now everything is about money, and everything is a negotiation. Hey, at least they'll be solid businessmen.

After the divorce, all of that went out the window for a while. When Daddy and "Le" bought the boys a trampoline, I immediately took them out to get the Xbox and the Nintendo Wii that I had sworn would never be inside my home. I knew that I would always be their only mother, but I feared that my sons would want to spend more time with their new family because of the fun, new gadgets, so I tried to compete. LeAnn would buy them everything under the sun, and I wanted to go tit-for-tat (or how about tit-for-tit, since she went out and got my exact fucking boob job?). I felt that I was competing with this woman for my children's love, and it felt even worse than losing Eddie. I know it sounds horrible, but it's how I felt. LeAnn had once told me in a bitter, anger-fueled text-off that she couldn't wait to meet my children, and once she did, she would would dote on them, make them lunches, drive them to soccer practice, and do all the other motherly duties that should have been reserved for me. She was simply making an ugly attempt to rattle my cage. But I just didn't want this new woman touching my babies.

The boys quickly learned to take advantage of the situation, and everything became a game. They were constantly trying to figure out what they could shake me down for. I would take them to the toy store or Target and let them go wild. Their eyes would beam with excitement as they ran up and down the aisles grabbing everything off the shelves. Once we got to the car, they would rip the boxes open, and for the next fifteen minutes I was the best mom in the whole world. The next day, I would find the toys lying in a corner of the room, where they would stay indefinitely. It was a quick fix. I was just throwing shit at these kids to make myself feel better, rather than doing something positive for my boys.

That's where Eddie and I both fucked up, because I knew he was doing the same thing. And I knew he felt the same way I did about it. We couldn't buy our children's affection. That's not what this was about, and they were learning to manipulate us against each other into getting what they wanted. We were drowning these children with these lavish, expensive gifts, and I simply couldn't afford it anymore.

The other shoe finally dropped when I told the boys we were flying up north to see their grandparents and their cousins, and they asked, "Are we flying private?"

"Are you fucking kidding me?" I thought. "You're little boys and you're asking me if we're taking a private jet to Sacramento?"

"No," I barked. "We're flying Southwest."

Instead of randomly showering the boys with presents, I decided to implement a program to make them work for their rewards. I'm aware this is far from a novel idea, but sometimes the simple lessons are the most difficult to learn. I decided to set up a chore-and-reward chart. For every good day, they would get one point, and once they reached ten points—meaning ten "good" days—they could trade that in for one $10 toy.

Okay, I know this seems like a lot of money for just behaving, but come on, people; this is Los Angeles, after all. If I offered them a quarter, they would just laugh at me, so I'm working with what I've got. It isn't the most earth-shattering advice, but it has worked well for my family, so far. When the boys earn enough to buy themselves a toy, I take them to the store to pick something out. They can only buy it if they can afford it, with not a penny from me. And guess what? They keep that toy at their hip for weeks.

It's easy to get caught up in the competition, but that wasn't what was important anymore. It took me a while to get there, but I was finally realizing what mattered most: our kids. Being a parent isn't easy. Being a single parent is harder. Being a single parent in Los Angeles is just about as tough as it gets.

While Eddie and I shared the same meager financial beginnings, we actually had very different familial environments. Eddie came from a conservative Cuban family; his parents maintained the traditional roles of husband and wife. His dad was a banker and his mom was an office manager/bookkeeper. My family was far from traditional. My mother was a free-spirited, braless hippie who gave me a graphic rendering of intercourse at a young age after I asked for it, and my dad, well, we already talked about the marijuana he grew in the backyard—both of which made me popular in high school. We were always naked in the house and taught from a young age to love and respect our bodies. So if I wasn't rocking my totally eighties gymnastics leotard, I was in a tiny dress. (Wearing lots of clothes has never been my thing—obviously.)

When it came time to start having difficult conversations with our oldest son, Eddie left it to me—and because my mother was open with me, it came easily. Yes, it can be awkward as hell to talk to your five-year-old about why it's inappropriate to show his penis to a female classmate, but these conversations need to happen.

Mason recently came home from his dad's house and announced, "Dad told me what *ho* means." My son was trying to get a temperature read on my reaction, but I didn't budge.

"Okay, Mase, what does it mean?"

"It's short for *hooker*," he said, a little proud of himself. Then he looked back at me. "What does *hooker* mean?"

Of course, Eddie had taken the easy way out. He answered Mason's question with something that would inevitably lead to more questions, but for Eddie, that was easier then actually confronting the issue. Just as my parents did with me, I try to tell the boys the truth whenever possible (except in the cases of both Santa Claus and divorce), but how does a parent explain prostitution to a nine-year-old?

"A hooker is a man or woman who will give a person a lot of physical attention in exchange for money," I said. "Most people consider this a bad thing, because it's not real and it's illegal to do this." Except in Vegas or Amsterdam.

I think Mason was a little underwhelmed with the answer and had expected it to be far more salacious, but he accepted it. He'll figure it out one day, but for now he knew the basics and was able to walk away understanding two important things about a word that should never be used by children: (1) its true meaning (at least the crux of it) and (2) that it wasn't socially acceptable.

I'm doing my best to appreciate my boys while they're still young. Children in Los Angeles grow up a lot faster than kids in other parts of the country, and I know it's only a matter of time before the boys are too embarrassed to give their mommy a kiss before school or hold her hand at the grocery store. I hear stories all the time of young children experimenting with drugs, and of parents overhearing their kids having graphic sexual conversations. How many tween starlets have been caught sending "sext" messages and naked photos? Looking back on my life, I thought even seventeen was a bit too young for me to be doing what I was doing, but today's children are doing that stuff in junior high school—and these kids are preteens! They should be having slumber parties and prank-calling their classmates . . . not smoking pot and having oral-sex parties.

But with so many absentee and self-involved parents in Hollywood, it's all too common and, unfortunately, a reality that I have to face. When children are left to their own devices, they will cry out for attention any way they can, and oftentimes it's by saying and doing things that are not only inappropriate, but also dangerous and illegal.

Luckily, Eddie and I have done a fairly good job of shielding the boys from a lot of the douchebaggery that comes with Los Angeles, but I am also going to be honest and forthcoming with my children when they ask me real questions. Filling them with nonsense isn't going to help anything.

When Mason wanted to go to sleepaway camp last summer, I decided it was time to have a conversation with him about what is appropriate and what is inappropriate behavior between an adult and a child.

I wasn't ready for him to go to sleepaway camp, and it became a larger issue between Eddie and me when I said no. At nine years old, I didn't feel he was prepared for situations that could be dangerous—whether it was sleepaway camp, day camp, or surf camp. I figured that if I started those important conversations now, he would be better prepared the following year . . . and so would I.

One afternoon when Mason was throwing a fit that he was the only one of his friends not going to sleepaway camp that summer, I decided we should have the discussion. We sat together on the floor of my kitchen and had an honest, sincere conversation, and one that I will cherish. Look, trying to explain rape and molestation to your kids is never easy, but if you don't prepare them, who will? Mason and I talked about the serious stuff. He asked questions and I answered the best I could. I told him that, most important, if anything happened, he would need to tell someone he trusted immediately. Even though someone taking advantage of him might fill his head with empty threats about hurting him or his family, that person was a bad person and Mason could always tell his dad or me. Nothing would happen to us, and the most important thing Mason could do was to speak up and immediately tell someone.

We live in a culture where no one speaks up, and I wish people would. For instance, why didn't someone at my wedding say, "Oh, yeah, I have a reason these two should not be joined in holy matrimony: he fucked half the cocktail waitresses in Hollywood." I would have applauded that person's candor—after crawling out of my hole.

Eddie was none too pleased with my decision to talk to Mason about molestation, but I stood my ground. I think sometimes Eddie fights with me because he feels he has to. Does he seriously expect me to believe that he would have preferred having that conversation with Mason himself? He didn't even have the wherewithal to properly explain to the boys the definition of *playboy* when he was on his short-lived NBC series.

Once again, Mommy had to do all the heavy lifting. I sat the boys down to talk to them about Mommy's and Daddy's jobs. I think that's important to do, regardless of your profession. As I mentioned earlier, the value of a dollar is lost on most children, so if they can better understand what you do every day when you're away from home, and that it allows you to keep food on the table and toys in the toy box, everyone is better served.

"Mommy and Daddy are both on TV shows," I said. "You can't watch either of them, because they are inappropriate for children. When you are older, you can watch them." The boys wouldn't understand watching their dad on television kissing another woman, and Eddie's show had a violence- and sex-fueled story line that was too adult for them, anyway. It would be confusing for the boys. It was even difficult for me to accept that Eddie was making out with other women for television shows and movies, but I had to remind myself that it was only acting. Did I ever tell you about this little made-for-TV movie he did called *Northern Lights*? I guess Eddie was a real Method actor. #JustSayin.

"Why would you do a show if it's inappropriate?" Mason asked. He's always one step ahead.

"Because that's the world we live in, Mason. It's a television show for grown-ups, and it helps Daddy pay his bills and it helps Mommy pay our bills."

Late last year, Eddie and I started a legal battle to determine whether the boys could be shown during background shots of *The Real Housewives of Beverly Hills*. My ex-husband is adamantly against the idea, but I am arguing that it is in all of our best interests. I'm by no means trying to exploit the boys or putting them directly in front of the camera, but simply in passing (like Adrienne Maloof's three kids). When we are shooting a season, I am constantly filming, and that restricts the time I have with the boys. If they can at least be around the cameras, that makes working so much easier. And as Eddie damn well knows, I need the money.

"Are you an actor?" Jake asked. Separating "reality personality" from "actor" is something the boys are still having a little bit of trouble with.

"No, honey, I'm not an actor. Mommy is just being herself on television."

"When we used to go out with Dad and Le, people used to take our photos all the time," Jake said. My sons had also gotten used to the paparazzi. At first it was exciting to them that people wanted to take their picture, but they quickly became numb to it. "Now when we go out with you, there are more photographers. Why is that?"

I was floored. I know children are sponges that absorb everything around them, but I would never have expected them to notice this, and I was not prepared with an answer. I wanted to blurt out, "I forgot to tell you that I got somewhat famous thanks to your dad, who brutally divorced me in front of the world and left me for a country singer. So your mom got a job on this really popular reality show, and your dad got a job on a lack-luster drama series that was canceled after four episodes. Oh, and karma's a bitch." But, alas, you can't say that to a kid. Plus, I've been told once or twice that I should think before I speak, so I held my tongue.

To this day, I'm pretty sure Jake believes that a play-boy is someone who lives in Chicago and gets to ride the Ferris wheel at Navy Pier.

To give credit where it's due, Eddie became an extremely hands-on dad during our divorce. He wasn't a hands-on parent while we were married, but once he was given scheduled times to be with the boys, the dad thing came naturally to him. He took them to baseball games and amusement parks; he took them out to lunch and to the movies. Relatively normal stuff, but the boys were so excited to be doing all these activities with Eddie. When they would come back to my house a few days later, their faces would light up as they told me about all the exciting things they did with their dad. It sincerely warmed my heart. I was so happy that they were developing this crucial relationship with their father. Eddie's father, Carl, was and is a loving parent, so I always knew Eddie had it in him.

Most men underestimate how much they enjoy being a father, until they no longer have the privilege all the time. As a parent, you take for granted that you can be with your children whenever you want, but when you're sharing them with someone else, it can be an eye-opening experience. I think sharing custody has its pros and cons. It sucks not having my kids whenever I want them. Sometimes, I'm having a bad day and all I need is to see Jakey's mischievous smile or feel one of Mason's bear hugs to bring me back to center. Splitting the holidays is also pretty rough, made even more difficult when you don't have a partner to share them with. I think the hardest thing is watching another parent figure enter their lives. It's something Eddie has yet to experience, but I can tell you firsthand that it's excruciating. Knowing that one day my sons might go to their bonus mom to ask for advice on a girl they like or for help with their algebra homework (as if she'd know how to do it, anyway), or even for something as simple as lunch money, is a wretched feeling. On the other hand, both Eddie and I have learned to value and appreciate the days we get with the boys, now that it's only half the year. And with part of my week free, I'm able to do things for myself, such as working, writing, shopping, etc. Because of my breakup, I discovered that I missed me time while I was married. I didn't give myself enough of it, and it's crucial. On the flip side, I think Eddie discovered that he really missed Dad time. We both finally established a better balance, and in a weird way, I think it has made us better parents.

Regardless of your marital status, religion, ethnicity, or sexual orientation, I think we can all agree that Los Angeles is one of the most difficult cities in which to raise normal, grounded children.

First of all, don't get me started on the Los Angeles Unified School District. As I said, my parents sent my siblings and me to private school, because the local public schools were simply too dangerous for us to attend. In Los Angeles, if you want to send your children to a high-rated public school, you have two options: be prepared to drop $10 million on a home in Beverly Hills proper (not Post Office, there is a difference! Just because it says 90210 doesn't mean you're actually in Beverly Hills) or pack up your family and move to Calabasas. Eddie and I chose the latter.

Most well-regarded private schools in Los Angeles cost about $20,000 a year. Are you kidding me? Basically, by the time your kid goes from kindergarten to twelfth grade, you've already dropped more than a quarter of a million dollars on his or her education—that's a fucking house in most towns. #LAProblems. Luckily, despite my move to Encino, the boys are still able to go to the public grade school near our old home. We don't have to worry about high school for a few more years yet, but I'm already psyching myself up to write a pretty staggering tuition check. (So please, lose this copy of my book and go buy a new one. Encourage all your friends to do the same.)

It isn't just the schools that come with the outrageous price tag; just about everything else in Los Angeles is subject to a West Coast markup. Some of you may have heard about a $50,000 Mad Hatter–themed birthday party for a four-year-old girl thrown by one particular Beverly Hills housewife. As atrocious as it might sound, it's not that uncommon.

The boys and I went to one birthday party in our old Calabasas neighborhood for a two-year-old boy at which the "event planner" had blocked off the entire cul-de-sac to create a race-car track. The birthday boy could barely walk, but he needed a fucking racetrack at his birthday? The dads sure did seem to enjoy it. Birthday parties here are almost always more for the parents than they are for the children. There's a certain need to impress and outdo one another: If one party had Buzz Lightyear show up, the next would have Buzz, Woody, and Mr. Potato Head appear. The gift bags alone cost a fortune. You're spending $10 to $15 a goodie bag for roughly thirty kids... and for what? To fill it with junk that most kids will likely toss to the corner of a room as soon as they get home? When it's all said and done, the kids don't give two shits. They just want to run around, scream, and eat cake.

For Mason's first birthday, I spent $10,000 on an incredibly lavish party—complete with an ice bar and margarita machines, costumed entertainers, and catered Texas BBQ. Mason slept through most of the festivities, but the nanny did trot him out for a few photo ops with his birthday cake. (Staged photo ops were something that would unfortunately become second nature for my little man.)

After my divorce, I could no longer afford the decadent birthdays the boys were so used to having, and I felt
guilty. For Jakey's fourth birthday party, we took over a
Chuck E. Cheese in the Valley, and I remember sweating
over having to split the bill with their dad. (Couldn't he
and his sugar mama have just picked up the check? I was
the one forced to sit there with a broken ankle, across
from his new wife and my former in-laws.) The following year, I decided to do my own thing and keep Jake's
birthday party low budget: a platter of peanut-butter-
and-jelly sandwiches, a grocery-store cake, and a few
bottles of wine and beer for the adults. And you know
what? I think it was the best party he ever had, because
there wasn't all this stress and anticipation. Instead, he
got to run around in the backyard like an animal with all
of his friends, jumping all over the swing set and playing games. Inside, the parents all appeared casual and
relaxed. Or maybe I just noticed it, because I finally was.

Raising a family in Southern California isn't all that
bad. Sure, I have to deflect a lot of the self-entitlement
and self-involvement that children often develop when
living so close to the world's most narcissistic city, but it

does offer some pretty amazing upsides for raising children, too.

There aren't many other places in the world where my boys can play baseball outside year-round or go to a different local theme park every weekend of the month. If they want to, Mason and Jake can go skiing in the morning and have a beach bonfire at night. They live active lifestyles and have extremely healthy diets for little boys (except for Mommy's occasional Del Taco run, my fast-food kryptonite). It's hard to ever be too depressed when it's warm and sunny pretty much every day of the year.

Sure, we don't have the change of seasons all the East Coasters commonly complain about, but Big Bear is only a few hours away, and there's this nice house off Mulholland that churns out fake snow during the holidays.

Speaking of Santa Claus, he's a particularly divisive character in the Beverly Hills area. (Perhaps it's his weight? Or maybe it's because no one in LA has worn a fur-trimmed jacket since the eighties?) You'd be better off talking about Scientology.

My ex-husband and I chose to raise our children Christian, but with so many Jewish friends in the area we

always joked that our children were "Cubish." We cele-
brated Hanukkah with our Jewish friends and Christmas
with our families. For us, it worked perfectly. I think the
Jews figured out a way better system than us Christians.
Christmas morning in our house was always absolute
chaos: wrapping paper flying in every direction, dozens
of toys being opened and discarded within moments, and
more triple-A batteries than could ever be appropriate.
Jewish people, on the other hand, give their children one
present per day. That way, kids can actually pause for
a minute and enjoy the gift, before eventually discard-
ing it and moving on to the next. When three-quarters
of your children's classmates are Jewish, try explaining
why Santa Claus doesn't go to their houses. Or better yet,
why Jewish parents are telling their children that Santa
isn't real. If you're a parent and you know your child's
classmate believes in Santa, why would you knowingly
burst his bubble? It's shocking how many parents try
to do this, so in typical grade-school form, I decided to
play dirty. "Well, Mason, Santa Claus doesn't go to every
little boy's and little girl's house. If you don't believe in
him and tell other kids not to believe in him, he flies
right by," I would say. "When you go back to school after

Christmas, ask your friend if Santa came to his house . . .
because I'll bet he didn't."

brandi's **babble**

Your kids only have one "Mommy." (Bonus ones need
not apply.)

CHAPTER NINE

His Future Ex

I often get the question "How do you deal with his new wife?" My answer is always the same: "How can I not?" I don't have a choice.

I would love to pretend that she doesn't exist. I've never been the biggest country-music fan, so it's not like I ever stumble across her songs on the radio. (I pretty much listen to all gangsta rap, all the time—its grittiness speaks to my roots. #GhettoBrandi) I would love to believe that when my children aren't sleeping under my roof that they are at their best friend's house or a fully vetted and safe spa retreat for children in the Valley. Maybe it's silly, but I'd just rather not dwell on the thought that my kids are sharing a home half the time with my ex-husband and his new wife.

I would love to believe that my ex-husband is miserable, overweight, bald, and alone. But that's not reality—at least not totally.

The short answer is, I deal with her for my kids. Through all of this, I wanted to spare them as much heartbreak and pain as I possibly could. She's good to them and they love her, so I try to be as civil as I possibly can. Sure, part of me gets angry thinking about her tucking my babies into bed at night in her home, when she and Eddie are the reason they no longer get to live with their mommy and daddy, but I have to learn to let that go. I'm not saying it will happen overnight, but in a blended family where cheating was involved, you will eventually need to let it go. I'm still working on the "forgive and forget" part, but its gets easier with time. To say it's been an uphill battle would be the understatement of the decade!

I do believe, though, that Eddie is slightly miserable in his new marriage (and possibly taking Propecia again. I mean, his hair seems to be doing quite well). I know it sounds like I'm just the bitter ex-wife hoping and praying that my ex-husband—who destroyed my heart and shattered my world—is unhappy with the woman he left me for. And now that I think about it, sure, that sounds about right. But I'm not just shooting from the hip; I'm looking at the hard facts. This man, who clearly has a weakness for the ladies, jumped from one "committed" (we'll use that term loosely) relationship to another. #Rebound. Marriage clearly doesn't mean a whole lot to this guy, and I think given his track record, wife number two has got to be all over him like white on rice. Knowing how their relationship developed, wouldn't she question every call he went to take privately or who was on the receiving end of his text messages?

Diving headfirst into a new marriage may not have been the brightest move. Sure, Eddie prefers to be in relationships, because he needs to feel that he's being taken care of. However, I'm pretty confident that my ex-husband would really have enjoyed taking some time to run around town banging twenty-year-olds left and right without having to look over his shoulder for the first time in almost a decade and a half. Additionally, I'm not sure he knew entirely what he was getting himself into with LeAnn. Was he prepared to take the backseat to her life and career? Eddie relished the spotlight while he had it. (Why else do you think he would agree to all those posed paparazzi shots?) I wonder if he'll be able to accept that it's his new wife who will always be the bigger draw.

I was forced to deal with their relationship way before I was ready. Between the countless celebrity-gossip websites and weekly magazines, it's sort of impossible to avoid their never-ending barrage of staged paparazzi shots. (My personal favorites are the perfectly posed yet impossibly candid photos of the happy couple cruising on a boat in Mexico, gazing off into the distance.) Photographers come with the territory when you're working in the entertainment industry—even I have learned to accept it and utilize it when necessary—and being rude to them won't get you anywhere. (No one wants to end up on the cover of *Star* without makeup.) So, while I understand the need to throw them a bone every once in a while, it seems slightly pathetic to keep pushing your stale love story down people's throats over and over.

The pictures can be hard to see—especially the shots of her with my children. Seeing my ex-husband's new wife playing bonus mom to my babies, the boys I gave birth to, was an absolute gut punch. Even worse was see-ing her inappropriately hanging all over Eddie, wearing virtually nothing, while my children were nearby watch-ing. I wanted to hurt this woman.

When she sent me those inappropriate text messages about her desire to "mother" my kids, I responded as most levelheaded mothers would: "Listen, bitch, you barely have my husband. I will kill you before you get your hands on my children." That is quite possibly the kindest thing I could have said to her, given the situation. I'm pretty sure she disagreed.

Occasionally we are forced to interact, but I try to avoid making any sort of eye contact with her. What can I say? I don't have a ton of respect for the woman, and I'm not that good at faking "nice." So on the rare occasion that she does address me and I am required to look at her, I make it as short and sweet as possible. If my children are around, I am always polite and try to excuse myself from the situation as quickly as possible. In an ideal world, I think LeAnn feels that maybe someday she and I could be friends. Well, in an ideal world she would have kept her legs shut and refrained from fuck-ing my husband (and he would have kept his dick in his pants). While I've been grateful for the overwhelming fan support I've received over the past few years, I've also had a good number of people criticize me for "blaming" the affair on LeAnn, because my beef should be with my husband. Don't worry, it is. #CheatersSuck. LeAnn didn't know me when they started messing around, so she didn't owe me anything (except maybe common decency). He was the one with a wife and two kids back at home. That doesn't mean I don't hold her partially accountable, though. My major issue with her was how she handled everything after the story appeared. She refused to take any ownership over her actions—even toward her own husband—and wouldn't accept any blame. Guess what? If you're going to play in the mud, you're going to get fucking dirty. #ChildStarSyndrome. Then our contentious relationship sort of escalated from there.

She has nice skin. That's the one compliment I can offer her—if forced. I'm assuming she spends a lot of time getting facials, but the amount of foundation she plasters on her face is obscene. She once arrived at a school performance with a full face of thick, caked-on makeup, a whole strip of false eyelashes, a perfect blow-out, and five-inch heels. Anyone who is insecure enough to rock that look at eight in the morning for a grammar-school Thanksgiving play has a boatload of issues. Look, I'm equally guilty of breaking out the big guns, but there is a time and a place for everything—and my son's school event is not one of them. #JustSayin.

I was never threatened by her. It gave me a strange sense of relief that Eddie hadn't shacked up with some Victoria's Secret model (although that might have required him to actually work for a living). Clearly, though, she was threatened by me. Not so much because of how I looked or acted, but because of my role in Eddie's life and the boys' lives. Why else would my ex-husband be banned from talking to me? I'm relegated to coparenting with him via his assistant? He never responds to e-mail, and my number is still blocked from calling his cell phone. How were we supposed to take care of our two children, if she erected this huge wall between us? We were clearly never reconciling, so I didn't understand the point (and still don't). All three of us needed to check our egos at the door if we were going to be good guardians to these two little boys.

About a year after Eddie and I separated, I decided that the three of us needed to find a way to coexist, and

I thought that perhaps blended-family therapy would help. It's a total LA cliché, isn't it? Have you ever heard of a family in Omaha going to "blended-family therapy"? For months, the three of us were jumping down each other's throats and triangulating the children. Mason's nightly phone calls to Dad became less like conversations and more like interrogations. So, therapy seemed the only reasonable—albeit ridiculous—solution to the problem.

"How about therapy?" I finally asked Eddie.

He took a minute to chew it over before responding, "Let me talk to LeAnn."

Eddie always hid behind a skirt, but I was surprised he didn't dismiss it completely (especially after seeing how ineffective our couples counseling proved). He is a traditional Latino man, and in many cultures therapy is considered a sign of weakness, so I wasn't sure if they would go with it.

A few days later, he sent me an e-mail saying that both he and LeAnn would be open to seeing a family therapist, if they chose the doctor.

"Ugh," I thought. Of course it had to be on their terms. I couldn't care less which doctor we went to, but

I had to make a little bit of a fuss about it before I even-tually conceded. Eddie told me that because I'm oh-so-willing to discuss personal matters with the press, he and LeAnn would need me to sign a confidentiality agree-ment before they would sit down in a room with me.

It took all my strength not to respond, "Right, because you both are soooo fucking famous that every newspaper in the world would be clawing for the story of what Eddie and LeAnn revealed during coparenting therapy." Are you fucking kidding me? It was laughable. I decided that at the end of the day, this was about being better people to one another so we could be better parents, so I agreed to sign the NDA.

It took a few weeks to get it lined up, but when I arrived at the doctor's office only a few minutes before our session, the lovebirds hadn't yet decided to grace the office with their presence. I had made it a point not to dress up for the appointment; I didn't want either of them to think I had any interest in trying to impress any-one. I came straight from my Pilates class in head-to-toe workout gear and a pair of flip-flops. Shortly after Eddie opened the door, his perfectly coiffed fiancée wobbled in on sky-high heels and with a full set of eyelashes. I was starting to get the idea that this was her typical morning uniform. I suppose it *was* almost lunchtime. Hindsight being twenty-twenty, I should have brought a glass of chardonnay.

Watching my ex-husband standing in front of me, comforting another woman and holding her hand, was probably one of the most surreal moments of my life. It was a strange sensation, because while it was extremely odd, I didn't feel jealous. I was finally numb to their entire existence. I simply didn't care. Since I signed away my right to speak, I can't reveal what was discussed when we finally stepped into the therapist's office, but I can share that it was an incredibly gratifying and vindicating experience . . . for me.

I've said it before and I'll say it again: child stars are a particular breed of hideous. Being surrounded by yes-men and yes-women all of your teenage and adult life will give people an altered sense of reality. They have this extreme sense of entitlement that they can have anything they want . . . including other people's husbands. When LeAnn set her sights on Eddie, she was relentless about getting him, and the damage her decision would cause never seemed to register.

Well, guess what? She won. I'll give her that. But she also won a marriage full of doubt, insecurities, and a perpetual voice in the back of her head saying, "Is he telling the truth?" If I could peer into a crystal ball, I imagine I would see an ever-growing list of canceled tours, concerts, and appearances in her future, for fear of leaving her husband home alone.

For that, I pity her.

As the saying goes, time heals all wounds. I can genuinely and sincerely say that I wish LeAnn nothing but the best, because hopefully once she gets happy with her life, she'll back the fuck out of mine. For the sake of our children, I hope her marriage to Eddie lasts a lifetime, because the ugliness that comes along with breakups and divorce isn't something I want my boys exposed to ever again. They care about her, and I don't want them experiencing any more loss in their lives. I wish that LeAnn would focus her energy back on her career, instead of dieting, suing people, tweeting, and wearing bikinis. After all, she is a talented woman with an amazing voice. Maybe she needs help remembering that sometimes, too. I cross my fingers that Eddie soon finds work as a regular on a television series. Even though I no longer get alimony from my ex-husband (only child support), I know that a working Eddie is a happy Eddie, and a happy Eddie equals a happy home for the boys. I hope that someday soon LeAnn will be blessed with children of her own. I think that her having her own baby might give her a much-needed reality check on what it means to be a mother and, perhaps, a little perspective on what I went through. I'm not meaning that to sound completely bitchy . . . just a little.

Maybe one day, far in the future, LeAnn and I will be able to put our differences behind us and develop some sort of friendship. I have this hysterical fantasy that one day she and I will decide to record a duet about heartbreak. I'm an expert on the subject, and if I pull out that crystal ball again, I have a feeling she may be an expert one day, too. I can't sing for shit, but that doesn't mean it won't be an iTunes sensation! However, I know that after publishing this book, I will most likely get slapped with yet another cease-and-desist letter from a certain country-music singer's legal team. I believe it will be lucky number three.

For the time being, she is a part of my life. She is my children's stepmother and someone I'm going to be forced to be around at soccer games, school recitals, and birthday parties. Do I want her to love and care for my children when they're with her? Of course I do. Do I have to like her? Fuck no, but I do have to deal with her.

brandi's **babble**

Never underestimate the impact of a properly timed "sloppy seconds."

CHAPTER **TEN**

I Will Survive

The Beverly Hills Police Department's holding cells were shockingly comfortable. I had only ever seen the inside of a jail on episodes of *Law & Order*, so I was pleasantly surprised by the amenities—which included a selection of the weekly magazines I so frequently appeared in those days. I'm not suggesting anyone try to get locked up; I'm just saying that it wasn't as horrible as I thought it would be. But it was still pretty horrible. I'm incredibly claustrophobic, and the small cells were giving me a panic attack (and obviously my Xanax was nowhere nearby). I was freaking the fuck out.

I was arrested on October 29, 2010, and charged with driving under the influence of alcohol. The officer turned on his sirens behind me after I had already arrived in the driveway of my then-boyfriend's home in Beverly Hills, just after midnight. After I refused to take a Breathalyzer test (advice from my brother, a Stockton CHP officer), the arresting officer spent about three minutes shining a bright flashlight in my eyes, before asking me to walk a straight line and then touch my finger to my nose. I mean, that's probably something I couldn't handle sober. I didn't feel drunk by any means, but clearly I was tipsy enough to alert this officer. I had consumed a few glasses of wine over three or four hours, sure I was a little buzzed, but at the time, I felt more than capable of driving.

Clearly, he was unsatisfied with my performance (and was sort of a dick in general), so I was booked at 12:45 a.m. We took the short drive over to the Beverly Hills Police Department, where I was half-hoping I would run into Eddie Murphy. As I was sobbing in the station, an overfriendly booking clerk took pity on me and attempted to lighten the mood when taking my photo by saying, "This is your official *TMZ* mug shot." She clearly had no idea that this really *would* be my official *TMZ* mug shot. She meant no harm, which I was grateful for, but her joke hit a little too close to home, and I started crying even harder—completely ruining any remains of my mascara. I knew it wouldn't take long for the media to catch wind of my arrest, and it would soon be on every celeb website from here to Timbuktu. Immediately, I thought about my boys: "Oh, no. What have I done?" I started to panic. How was I going to explain this to my children? How about my parents, who'd bent over backward to help me get a fresh start? And I could only imagine the lecture I was going to get from my ex-husband. I spent the next eight hours listening to someone throwing up a few cells down and having sporadic attacks of severe claustrophobia. I killed time by perusing the list of names carved into the wall, searching for anyone recognizable. Alas, I couldn't find Paris, Nicole, or even Lindsay. I was feeling really alone.

Despite the fine alleged on the police report, I never paid a dime for bail. With no prior criminal record, the booking clerk released me at 8:30 the next morning. The only real punishments would be the utter humiliation and a court-mandated Breathalyzer. It was to be installed in my Range Rover, and I was required to blow into it before my engine would start. That's it. I literally walked right out of the police station.

I found my billionaire boyfriend circling the building in total confusion—this was clearly his first dalliance with the BHPD. We drove back to his house, and I was relieved to find my car still parked in the driveway. Since I was technically on private property when I was pulled over, the police couldn't impound it. Ladies and gentlemen, welcome to Brandi Glanville's Drunk Driving 101. First of all, don't drink and drive. It's just not worth it—trust me. Second, if you're an idiot (as I was) and get pulled over, make sure you pull onto a driveway of someone you know. It will save you a fortune in impounding charges.

I'm not quite sure this was even legal for me to be driving just hours after my DUI, but I immediately jumped into my car and behind the wheel—still in my lamé leggings and faux-fur vest—and headed to Jake's preschool Halloween parade. Despite the fact that I was driving, it was a complete walk of shame. This was officially my rock bottom.

It was time for me to grow the fuck up. Even if it was just a couple of glasses of wine, I recognized that I had been indulging for way too long. It was time to figure this shit out and clean myself up. Seriously, what was so important that I thought it was a smart idea to get behind the wheel of a car? I truly believe that God was looking out for me that night. I think he was offering me the dramatic wake-up call I so desperately needed.

I needed to understand that I had somehow stumbled upon a sliver of tabloid fame, and now my actions and fuck-ups would be made available for the world to read about. They would be filed away, so that one day my boys could dig them up. I needed to be an adult . . . for my kids and for myself. I royally fucked up. I was beyond lucky that getting pulled over in a driveway was the extent of my punishment for drinking and driving. I was so fortunate that no one got hurt. What if I had hit another car? What if someone was hurt or, God forbid, killed because I made a terrible, stupid decision? Talk about not being there for my kids. How could I be there for my kids, if I was spending years upon years in jail because of a reckless decision I made one night? I needed to figure my shit out . . . immediately. I had spent a year and a half in a total fucking tailspin, and guess what? I needed it. My life had shattered around me, and I needed to fall off the deep end for a while.

Sometimes you need to lose yourself to truly find

yourself again. But at the end of the day, you have to know when to wake the fuck up and get on with your life. When I had the "drive of shame" to my son's school, I knew that it was my time. I had to snap the fuck out of it. I had allowed myself to go crazy, but now it was time to fall back in line. It was time for me to invest in life's three core therapies: Hypno, Beauty, and Retail.

Shortly after my DUI, I started seeing a hypnotherapist to help cure my face-picking addiction. It sounds crazy, right? I needed therapy so I would stop tearing open the blemishes on my face. A close friend of mine suggested I meet with famed hypnotherapist Kerry Gaynor—apparently Dr. Gaynor had cured my friend of his cigarette addiction after just three sessions. After I was finally able to snag an appointment, Dr. Gaynor immediately diagnosed my face picking as a form of self-mutilation and that it would take far more than three sessions.

He said the picking was a symptom of the greater stresses in my life—but seriously, it doesn't take a degree in psychology to figure that out. We spent about five sessions diving into my skin issues, and I learned of a few contributing factors to my addiction. (1) Early in my modeling career, I was told that I was a body girl, not a face girl. I don't care who you are, that's going to fuck with most people. (2) At thirty-eight years old, I was just returning to the dating scene, in a city that prides itself on youth. And finally, (3) I have crazy-ass control issues. When my kids aren't around and I have too much time on my hands, I pick out of boredom. It allows me to forget about the other stressors in my life for a time, because I become obsessed with digging needles into my face. After the fifth session, Dr. Gaynor suggested I have a burial for my tweezers and needles. I'm sure there's some emotional significance, but I felt like an asshole burying my beauty tools in the backyard. Today, I'm allowed to have tweezers again, but not any needles. Keeping needles—or any other sort of weapon—away from most scorned women is probably a smart decision for everybody involved.

Once we got a good handle on the picking, Dr. Gaynor began asking me about other issues in my life. I think dealing with my face-picking addiction opened up the floodgates to the world of shit I had been swimming in. We started talking about my DUI arrest and my increased drinking since the divorce; we talked a little bit about my newfound trust issues with men and the occasional bouts of depression. We even spent some time talking about how I can better coexist in a world with LeAnn. I'm no longer allowed to google either LeAnn or my ex-husband.

My obsession with them was not out of jealousy or spite. I decided to divorce Eddie after discovering he was having a second affair (I'm a serious fool for not leaving him after the first one). He would never have left me otherwise. I chose this life. It wasn't an easy decision, but it was mine. When it came to Eddie and LeAnn, I was more concerned with my children. My ex-husband and I rarely communicate. I am blocked from ever calling his cell phone, and not until recently was I finally given a home phone number for him and LeAnn (it only took them two years), so it could be really difficult getting ahold of my kids. I would occasionally start to panic after not hearing from them for a day or two, so I would turn to Google to try to find where they were—just so I could rest assured that they were still breathing. As part of our custody agreement, I needed to be able to contact the boys while they were with their father, but for a while I was only given the number for their magicJack—a phone service that connected through their Internet. This allowed them to follow the court ruling inexpensively and easily without giving me a landline or a cell-phone number. This service only worked when the computer was on, which was never.

Dr. Gaynor said that my issues—from the face picking to the paralyzing fear of flying to the obsessing over my children—were all symptoms of my greater need to be in control. At the end of every session, he would lull me into deep relaxation and chant some affirmations. I saw him for two years, until, from his point of view, I was cured. However, I do keep one of his voice-mail messages saved on my phone, because just hearing his voice soothes me. I like to think he enjoyed our conversations, because I can't imagine he gets too many patients as candid as me.

I was dealing with my head and heart; now it was time to deal with the outside. Sometimes it's easy to just stop trying, isn't it? But we're not doing anybody any favors if we don't take care of ourselves.

Since I was able to curb the picking, I decided to focus on healthier ways to make me feel confident about my skin. My list might seem extensive, but I assure you, each procedure is completely necessary for me. Once a month, I treat myself to an IPL (intense pulsed light) photofacial to help reduce brown spots and acne scars. Every other month, I go in for a more intense laser therapy called Perfecta. I give myself weekly Jessner lactic acid peels to rejuvenate my skin and tighten my pores. Botox has been a part of my life for nearly fifteen years—today I am getting it in my forehead, around my eyes, and for the bunny lines around the bridge of my nose. I also dabble in fillers (both Juvéderm and Restylane) for my smile lines, the lines around my lips, my acne scars, and my nose.

Right after Eddie and I split up, I got fillers in my cheeks but absolutely hated it. I was totally unrecognizable. I'll never do it again. Once I did this ultrasound therapy called Ultherapy to tighten up my jawline and neck, but it hurt like a motherfucker, and I'm not even sure it worked. Plus, given my allergy to most pain medication, I got to feel every moment of torture. But I like it to hurt. I want to feel it working, so I know I'm getting my money's worth. Now I know this seems just like a continuance of my self-mutilation, but Dr. Gaynor can assure you that it's not. Promise!

Contrary to popular belief, I'm an eater: fried foods, pasta, hamburgers, cheese, guacamole, chips, hot dogs . . . you name it. You'll never find me ordering a piece of dry fish with a side of steamed broccoli. I was blessed with a speedy metabolism (don't hate me, I promise I was born with many other flaws), so when I was younger, I had a difficult time keeping on the weight (it sounds like champagne problems, but trust me, it was just as annoying then as trying to lose weight is now). I lived in Milan for most of my modeling years, so I developed an obsession with Italian food, Italian clothes, and Italian men. All the calories I consumed from the fresh mozzarella, fried calamari, and veal Milanese were burned during evenings with Paolo, Gundem, and Mossimo (to name a few).

Today, I have become diligent about working out. For me, Pilates is the best way for me to maintain my figure—long, lean, and strong—but it's different for everyone. I like Pilates because it lets me exercise while lying on my back. #Lazy. Experts always say that the most important thing is just getting off the couch, even if it's just to go for a walk. Bullshit. My eighty-five-year-old grandma goes for power walks that would put most people to shame, so don't tell me you can't aim a little higher. If you are under the age of sixty-five and not suffering any serious medical condition, get yourself to the gym—walking alone is not going to get you a twenty-five-year-old-looking ass. The only thing that will do that is intense exercise that gets your heart rate going. If you get bored chugging away on the elliptical, you can always opt to have a lot of rowdy sex instead.

When I'm going through a particularly rough time, the next step is to go shopping. They don't call it retail therapy for nothing, people. Whether it's $100 or $100,000, set aside some money to indulge yourself. I call it "the come-fuck-me fund." It's the quickest way to get a much-needed pick-me-up.

It doesn't take a fortune to look like a million bucks. Growing up, I would head to all the high-end stores and scout out that season's trends before heading to more cost-effective shops to put together similar looks. Fashion does not need to be expensive, but if you have the cash to burn, by all means drive immediately to Neiman Marcus.

For you ladies, invest in some fabulous basics. You

know your best assets, so don't be afraid to show them off. Whether it's an hourglass figure, head-turning cleavage, a high, cute derriere, or legs for days, make sure that you work what your mama gave you.

1. Jeans: Women today don't wear "mom jeans," they wear skinny jeans! Throw away those baggy, acid-wash Eddie Bauers and treat yourself to some great low-rise, skinny jeans. Sears stores across the country used to offer customers the opportunity to design their own Levi's. Old Navy does the same. It's a great way to custom-create a pair of jeans perfectly suited to your body. And remember, the higher and smaller the pockets, the higher, firmer, and cuter the booty. You can quote me.

2. Black sport jacket and white top: Nothing pairs better with a great pair of jeans then a formfitting blazer and white tee. The blazer should have just the slightest shoulder pad and a tapered, short waist (to show off those small, high pockets), and for me, I prefer a

body-hugging wife-beater. You can also pair the jacket with a men's button-down, with the top few buttons left open. It's a classic look that is both sexy and powerful. And that's sort of the whole point, isn't it?

3. Sexy heels: Every woman should own a pair of basic, black, pointy-toed heels. The look never goes out of style because it looks good on everyone. Plus, it's a surefire way to make you feel sexy as hell.

4. Black bra: The final element is a black bra. I don't want to see any women rocking this outfit with a boring nude bra. I want to see lace, frills—hell, I would even be open to some bedazzling. It's meant to be a little naughty underneath all that nice.

brandi's **babble**

Have more fun than you can handle, but always be the one in control.

CHAPTER **ELEVEN**

A Billionaire Saved My Life

Like the old saying goes, the best way to get over someone is to get under someone else. Well, I'm fantastic at that game. After a thirteen-year leave of absence, both my vagina and I were returning to the dating world feeling, in a way, reborn (mine was more of a figurative rebirth, while my vagina . . . well, that was chapter 6).

In some ways "dating" was an entirely different beast from what it was when I was last single, but in other ways, it was completely the same. The same fundamental rules apply—don't be too available; don't be a stalker; and don't give away the milk for free (unless you don't care if you see that person again)—but it's their application that has shifted. I needed to reeducate myself on the ways of the dating world, so here's what I learned. . . .

As I talked about earlier, social media is the largest indicator of whether someone is available. Since we can easily google just about everyone we meet, we're quickly able to identify some key facts about him—and usually determine right away whether that person is single. Before, it used to be whether that person had a ring on his finger (or a tan line where it normally is, for the really shady types. #JustSayin) or purposefully starting a conversation with "Well, my wife and I . . ." as a way to clue you in.

Facebook, Twitter, and all the rest have made stalking a potential love interest exponentially easier. It used to be that you would just call his or her house every few hours and hang up before the message machine clicked on, until you finally got through! Who needed to know that you had been calling every hour on the hour? #NotHot. Today, that is (a) totally unnecessary, because you can go on Twitter to find out exactly where that person is at any given moment (and with whom!), and (b) who has a landline with a message machine anymore? If you called that person's cell phone ten times in a day, he or she would have ten missed calls from you. And that's just #CrazyTown.

Speaking of cell phones, they have completely changed the rules of communication when dating. It used to be that a person had three days to call you after getting your phone number, and as the recipient, you had to wait at least twenty-four hours before returning the call. Well, I think that logic can be completely thrown out the window. The three-day rule was first invoked because it would cause the person waiting for your call to assume you were busy (out of the house, not near a phone) and not overly eager. While the principle still applies, who today doesn't have a phone on him or her at all times? I'm sorry, but the "I've been too busy to call" excuse just doesn't work anymore—especially in LA. Everyone sits in traffic, so everyone has time to call.

The twenty-four-hour response is also no longer applicable. If you wait more than a day to respond to someone, it gives the impression you are uninterested (because you most likely are). Today, it's assumed that you know the very moment someone calls, texts, or e-mails (and certain smartphones can even tell you if your text message or e-mail has been delivered and read). Generally no one is without his or her cell phone for more than three hours, so if you are interested, I think the three-hour rule is a good place to start.

Also, "sexting" is still sex. Okay, not really, but I think it's important to point out that if you're sending dirty text messages or having naughty FaceTime/Skype-time before he or she takes you on at least a second date, it's still giving away the goods for free. It's tempting to have a few glasses of wine and to start sending photos of yourself in sexy lingerie, but by all means, resist that temptation. Haven't we already learned enough lessons from former Disney starlets?

I've been back in the dating world now for a little more than three years, and I've already made some major mistakes and learned some valuable lessons. Here are a few more rules for getting back in the saddle:

1. Do not have more than two drinks and then expect to make a good decision. If I have learned anything through this journey, it's that men look much better after two drinks, and they might as well be Mark fucking Wahlberg after three. Everything looks better through wine goggles.

2. Just because he offers to pick you up does not make him a gentleman. How a person acts when he walks you to your front door is what determines whether he is a gentleman. I've found that a date will oftentimes offer to pick me up, purely so he can try to attack me as I reach my front door at the end of the night (figuring my bed isn't that far away).

3. Don't ever meet at his house. It's just a ploy—not too thinly veiled. If at all possible, meet your date out—whether it's at a restaurant, bar, or theater.

4. Always drive yourself. While taking a cab may seem like a good idea, it's also an easy excuse to have too many cocktails (see rule number 1). Especially if it's a first date! It will prove an invaluable tool in keeping the notches on your bedpost to a minimum. (If you're single and living in a relatively big city, I'm sure you've already lost count anyway . . . and good for you!) Plus, most people won't

ask you on a second date if you've given up the goods on the first date.

5. Never ask someone out over text messaging or social media. If you are on the receiving end of this sort of ask, do not respond. It may be 2013, but if someone wants to ask you out, he should have the balls to call you.

6. If you have children, do not introduce them to every person you date. While this should go without saying, I've witnessed count- less friends make this major mistake. I have been in a serious relationship with only one person since my divorce (and you'll soon see how that turned out), and that was the only person I ever thought of allowing to meet my children. Children are vulnerable and get attached quickly. If you've already split up from your child's mother or father, you do not need to bring more people into his or her life who will eventually disappear. Kids get con- fused with a revolving door of partners. And if you're bringing a revolving door of partners

around your kids, you might be pretty confused yourself.

When it comes to your children, dating new people is
a slippery slope. It's difficult balancing two separate lives,
and it's difficult deciding when is a good time to begin
integrating the two. But introducing someone to your
kids is a huge step. I have had a ton of microrelationships
and one serious one, but I have yet to introduce any man
to my boys (besides male friends whom I may or may not
fuck, if I get lonely or have too many glasses of wine—
but they're not going anywhere).

Ultimately, dating again reminded me that I was
an individual and not the forgotten half of an "almost
famous" couple. It allowed me to develop the self-
confidence I needed to move past my ex-husband, deal
with the pain of our split, and meet someone worthy of
my brand-new vagina.

It wasn't about the money.

Okay, maybe a little bit.

Three months after Eddie moved out, a friend of a

friend asked me if I would be interested in a blind date. I wasn't dating yet and was a bit hesitant. She prefaced it with "He's so not your type, but he's really smart and you'll have a good time." For most people, that would have been an immediate turnoff. I mean, it was the international code for "unattractive": "He's got a great personality."

For me, it was just what I needed—a nonintimidating first date that I wasn't invested in. It seemed like the perfect opportunity to get back on the bike, and the guy, Michael, could serve as a nice pair of training wheels. If she had said, "He's this hot Latin actor with abs you want to lick honey off of," I would probably have declined. Instead he was a shorter, older Jewish man who had made his fortune in real estate development.

"Okay," I conceded. "Where should I meet him?"

Michael asked to meet me at Dan Tana's, in West Hollywood—an iconic Italian eatery that I had always been dying to try. I must have asked Eddie more than a dozen times to take me to Dan Tana's, but he never wanted to leave the Valley (he was probably terrified we'd run into one of his girlfriends). I decided to meet a girlfriend beforehand for a drink at the Four Seasons

Beverly Hills. This was my first real date in thirteen years, and I was in need of some liquid courage, even to meet a guy I was certainly not going to be interested in. Before I knew it, I was already twenty minutes late for my date! My friend and I got so caught up with gossiping that I completely lost track of time. When I finally found my way to the restaurant, I immediately noticed the commanding-looking, handsome man in his early fifties, who was approximately two inches shorter than me. My friend was right: he was definitely not my usual type, but to be gracious, I decided to check "my type" at the door and be open-minded about this guy.

We sat there for three hours laughing, drinking, eating, and having the loveliest evening. I quickly realized that Michael wasn't just any old chump; he was one of the most powerful real estate developers in the country, and he had a Rolodex that would impress most studio executives. Plus, he had a wicked sense of humor and was exceptionally bright, which is hard to find and would normally have intimidated me, but he was easy to have a conversation with. When he finally walked me to the valet, he gave me a long hug and we said good-bye. Despite our having a great time, I never expected to hear from him again. He was fantastic, but he just wasn't my type—even with the homes around the world and the celebrity friends—and I thought I made that clear. I wasn't looking for a payday; I was looking for the butterflies again.

Over the next few weeks, I heard from Michael nearly every day asking me on some extravagant date or another. He was definitely interested, and he was going to pull out all the stops—and for a guy with endless means, they can be quite tempting. First, he asked me to join him for an LA Lakers home game, because, of course, he has impossible-to-get floor seats next to superproducer Jerry Weintraub, just a few seats away from Jack Nicholson. Then it was a weekend at his private residence in the luxurious El Dorado resort community in Cabo San Lucas (which, of course, he'd developed) or his waterfront home in Kauai. I politely declined all his invitations for weeks, but he was relentless, and that was a little intoxicating. I hadn't been pursued like that in years. One day, I got an e-mail from him asking me to go down to the Bahamas to visit the community and golf course he was developing there. My gut instinct was to decline again, but I thought, "Hey, I don't have the kids this weekend and could use a vacation." I decided to finally take him up on his generous offer, but I made it clear I would need my own room. He was a little taken aback by my directness, so I told him, "Look, I would love to go, but if you want to ask me, call me." We had a lovely phone conversation—one of our few, as he was the king of e-mails—in which I told him that I would be happy to go along for the ride, but I would need my own room. He told me that he would have to change some stuff around, but that it was totally fine. (I later found out that no woman had ever asked for her own room before—making me exponentially hotter in his eyes.) Then he told me his driver, Lucas, would follow up later that week with the details.

Lucas let me know that he would be fetching me at 9:00 a.m. on Saturday morning and taking me out to Van Nuys Airport for a 10:00 a.m. wheels-up departure time on Mr. Meldman's private plane. "Ugh," I thought. "Of course he has a private plane." In LA it always feels as if the more expensive someone's toys are, the more that person is overcompensating for something else. I didn't know Mike well at the time, but confidence didn't seem to be something he was lacking.

The idea of being trapped on a tiny jet for hours feeling every bump and change of direction was a paralyzing fear of mine. Over the next few days, I worked myself up over the flight and actually prepared to cancel on him more than once. By the time Saturday came along, I was prepared with a Xanax bottle the size of Texas.

When we finally got to the airport, I was fucking gobsmacked. This wasn't some tiny little propeller plane. This was a huge, beautiful airplane—a real-deal jetliner. I was still nervous about flying, but was comforted because this was a much bigger plane than I had imagined, and it was Mike's personal jet (not some NetJets fractional rental), with a pilot and a flight attendant who worked solely for him. Once I boarded the plane, I realized it wasn't just the two of us headed down to paradise; we were also flying with Mary Hart and her husband, Burt Sugarman.

Okay, I have been around some A-list celebrities and Hollywood power players, but Mary Hart? I was officially starstruck. I know it sounds superlame, but my mom absolutely adored Mary Hart, and I grew up watching her every day on *Entertainment Tonight*. I immediately sat down and started chatting with her.

I was determined to make her my pal, and we immediately became such good friends that by the time we took off, she was holding my hand to help get me through my mini panic attack.

After I finally calmed down, Mike alerted the flight attendant that we were ready for breakfast and, of course, some of the finest rosé champagne money could buy. "Hmm," I thought. "He's getting cuter by the minute!" We landed in the Bahamas in just five short hours because, naturally, we didn't have to stop for fuel and received permission to fly straight onto the island and into the resort—which was simply breathtaking.

We were shown to our luxurious five-star "tents" (translation: the most gorgeous rooms I'd ever seen) directly on the beach. It felt magical, perhaps even romantic. Once we settled in, Michael took us on a tour of "his" property, including million-dollar beachfront homes. Since I live in Los Angeles and have traveled the world, it takes a lot to impress me. I was thoroughly impressed, especially watching all the staff scurrying around to wait on Michael hand and foot. It was totally intoxicating, and I was starting to become attracted to this man. (Ladies and gays, power is sexy!)

That evening at our group dinner and three glasses of rosé later (yes, I broke my own rule), I realized I might not need that separate room after all, but I would resist temptation that first night. After the meal, he walked me to my "tent" and I invited him inside for a drink. We started making out like teenagers and kissed for a good hour before I finally sent him back to his own room. #PlayingHardToGet. By the time the next evening rolled around, let's just say I didn't need my own accommodations anymore. It was on . . . like Donkey Kong.

That's how our relationship continued for the next few months. Over time, I grew to depend on him as my voice of reason. He would advise me on career decisions and give me the confidence I needed throughout my divorce (he had already been through two of his own), and I was beyond grateful for his help. Finally, a man I could rely on. For about eight months, it was absolute perfection. Every day he lifted me up, telling me how young and beautiful I was. It had been a long time since a man I cared about had offered me that kind of validation; it was exactly what I needed to get my swagger back. He took me to swanky, glitzy events, where I could dress up in glamorous gowns and rub elbows with Cindy Crawford. (After a few glasses of wine, I might have gushed to Cindy about the picture we took together during our modeling days in Europe and asked for a fresh one, because the other one is twenty years old. #Just Sayin.)

For Michael, it was perfect, too: I was still legally married, spent half of my time with my children, and wasn't looking for a full-blown commitment from him. As time went on, my insecurities got the better of me, though, and I started to become . . . clingy. I started asking that he refer to me as his "girlfriend" and began demanding more of his time.

Despite the straining of our relationship, Michael took me to see his breathtaking private ski resort, the Yellowstone Club, in Big Sky, Montana. (Yes, ladies and gays, the man owns a mountain that the residents—aka movie stars and producers with gazillion-dollar mountainside cabins—call Private Powder.) One night during a group dinner, I started hinting to my new BFFs (in my head) Mary and Cindy that I was considering introducing Michael to my boys. We had been together for a while, and Michael was an important part of my life, so perhaps it was the right time.

"No, don't do that," Cindy quickly blurted out. Her response took me by surprise, and I immediately understood that she was privy to some information I hadn't known until now: I wasn't the only woman in Michael's life. He appeared to be noodling just about every good-looking girl in town. This guy whom I was so dismissive of when we'd first met was apparently an incredible ladies' man.

I was hurt, but I didn't blame him; we never discussed the exclusivity of our relationship. When we returned home, I could feel him start to pull away. He became increasingly unavailable, and our relationship started to dissolve. I learned about another model he was dating who had a reputation for being, well, batshit crazy, and it drove me nuts.

"Well, two can play this game," I thought. It was time for me to see other people, too. I burned quickly through a handful of actors and a few hot hockey players, while still spending time with Michael. I never told him I was dating other people, but he wasn't stupid. Unfortunately for me, it didn't seem to bother him. There was no more wining or dining, and eventually, I was reduced to being purely his sex slave and late-night booty call, when he found himself alone.

Michael took me on lavish vacations and took me out for decadent meals, but when it came to gifts . . . cheap! For Valentine's Day, I had bought him an extremely expensive Chrome Hearts belt (what do you get the man who has everything?), so he turned around and bought me a beautiful Bottega Veneta purse, but that was the only time he ever gave me anything (not that I'm not thankful for the amazing trips), and mostly because he felt obligated. Listen, I don't need a man to shower me with gifts, but I did want to feel that I was being wooed—at least a little bit. After nearly a year together, we officially broke up on my thirty-eighth birthday, in November 2010. We spent the evening together, but he didn't bother to get me any sort of gift or even a card and wanted to be in bed by 9:00 p.m. Way to make a girl feel special! I finally had enough and called it quits. I will always have love for him.

Around the same time, my divorce was becoming increasingly painful, and I was completely heartsick. Only this time, it wasn't about Eddie. Before Michael,

I wondered if I could ever love somebody again. My ex-husband had done such damage to my heart that I was sure I was scarred forever. It was strange: I was actually happy to feel that kind of pain. It made me feel alive again. Hurting over another man taught me that it was possible for me to find happiness again after my divorce. Michael was never meant to be the next great love of my life or the man I would one day grow old with, but he served an important purpose. He got me over Eddie.

CHAPTER **TWELVE**

A New Housewife

My first thought was, "Could I really be a 'Housewife' without a husband . . . or a house?"

When Evolution Media (the production company behind *The Real Housewives of Beverly Hills* and *The Real Housewives of Orange County*—and a trillion other hit shows) came to me in July 2010 to discuss the idea of my joining the *Beverly Hills* cast, I was over the moon about the possibility, but doubtful that anything would actually come of it. My luck wasn't the best during those days.

Despite its size, Los Angeles can be a small city. Rumors had been circulating for a few months that the show was looking to cast new members, and everyone wanted in. Adrienne Maloof and I had a handful of friends in common, but had never actually met until we were both on the red carpet of a charity event in Hidden Hills. Photographers asked us to pose for a few shots together, during which she asked me to hold her new puppy, Jackpot. For some reason, the photos went viral, and every blog was speculating that I was going to be joining the *Housewives* cast. A few days later, I got the call from Jennifer Redinger at Evolution asking if I would be interested in coming in for a camera test.

On a hotter-than-normal day in the Valley, I headed toward a production office near the Burbank Airport to meet with the casting team. Being absolutely awful with directions and still unable to program the navigation system in my car (#TechnologicallyChallenged), I had no idea where I was. Already late, I frantically dialed the casting producer to tell her I was lost and asked if she could help me with directions. I was actually there, only one parking lot over. I don't think I could have been more embarrassed.

It was early in the day, but I was dressed to the nines in a sexy Burberry dress (that I'd had shortened, naturally), five-inch Christian Louboutin heels, and every fancy piece of jewelry I owned. After all, I was supposed to be representing the 90210. Over the years, I had been on countless model castings and met some of the bitchiest fashionistas of all time. They'd treated me completely like shit, so I was prepared for the worst when I walked into that room. You can imagine my surprise when everyone was as nice as could be. I guess in those days, I was constantly preparing myself for the worst.

Jennifer asked me to take a seat in front of a camera and started asking me questions. I was petrified, but I did my best. If I came across particularly nervous during an answer, she would stop me and ask me to do it over. Maybe she was this nice to everyone, but I felt that she was rooting for me. To this day, I credit the producers of that show for changing my life—one in particular, Alex Baskin. I jokingly refer to him as the "housewife whisperer" for all the bullshit and drama he has to deal with. Between *Orange County*, *Beverly Hills*, and all of his other shows, he's got a lot of diva personalities to handle, and if any of us have a problem or a complaint, we run immediately to him. In that regard, I do not envy his job. I could tell from the first time we met that he felt sorry for me. He saw that I had been broken, and I could tell he wanted to fix it. And he did.

When I began my *Housewives* journey, I was still recovering from my divorce, and I looked to the show as an opportunity to reinvent myself, if I was given the chance. At first, I didn't think it was going to happen. I would read online about all the other amazing people they were interviewing and pour myself a drink. I thought I was never going to be that lucky, but I would still lie in bed daydreaming about how amazing it would be if I had my own voice and how much my life would change, if I could just get cast on this show. (I also fantasized about having people ask me for my autograph. I'm not sure why, but it sounded cool.)

I wanted to shed all the negativity in my life. I had adopted this bitter-Brandi persona, and in the press I still looked like the scorned ex-wife. I was desperate to extract myself from the D-list love triangle that I was entrenched in for the better part of three years, and I was eager to redefine myself. I wanted a fresh start.

One of my closest friends said to me, "Brandi, I can't wait for the day when we google your name and there is no reference to Eddie or LeAnn. And better yet, I can't wait for the day when you google LeAnn Rimes and your face pops up."

"Ha," I said. "Yeah, right!" I believed my sad little story would haunt me for the rest of my life—just like the HPV. The gifts that keep on giving.

After several interviews, months and months went by. I didn't hear a thing from the producers, so I chalked it up as another loss. Things weren't going so well for me at the time. A few weeks prior, I had broken my ankle and leg in a horrendous "walking accident." That's right, I was walking in sky-high stilettos and I tripped. It was the least glamorous and klutziest injury in the history of broken ankles, but I owned it.

Right before the show was set to begin filming its second season, I got a phone call on a Tuesday evening in the spring.

"Is this Brandi?" asked a sweet, high-pitched voice.

"Yes, this is she," I said cautiously. Occasionally, I was on the receiving end of some prank phone calls when my number got out, so I was always a little guarded.

"This is Sally-Anne King from *The Real Housewives of Beverly Hills*," she chirped. "We were wondering if you'd be interested in coming to a party tomorrow night and being on camera?"

"Of course," I said immediately. And that was it.

I didn't even ask her for any details because I didn't want to press my luck. I did, however, have to figure out what the hell to do about my broken foot. My friends told me I should cook up some tall tale about heli-skiing or horseback riding to tell the girls on camera—something that sounded exciting and posh. "Why would I do that?" I asked. "There's enough pretension on that show without me. I think I'd rather just keep it real with my new 'friends.'"

That night, I hobbled into the bathroom, grabbed my Chanel face-mask pot, and plopped onto the side of the bathtub. I wanted to look impossibly fresh for my first day of filming. I remember sitting there looking at the Ambien perched on the bathroom counter. Balancing on my crutches, I knocked the bottle into an open drawer and pushed it shut. Finally, things were looking up for me. I had something to look forward to, so I knew I wasn't going to need any help. There would be more sleepless nights ahead, I was sure of it, but for the first time in a long time, I was going to have a good night's sleep.

* * *

If you have ever watched any of the shows in the *Real Housewives* franchise, you already know that Bravo doesn't define *housewife* in the traditional sense—and for that I'm grateful. When Bethenny Frankel joined *The Real Housewives of New York* cast in 2008, she was a single entrepreneur living in an Upper East Side rental. Today's "housewife" is a sassy, clever, opinionated woman who faces challenges head-on and never shies from telling it like it is—all while hoping to create a happy "home life," regardless of what kind of home she has and who lives there.

Oftentimes, people's demeanor or attitude will change as soon as the camera's On light flickers. It's not as if I were revealing something hugely profound; a kindergartner could probably draw the same conclusion. It's like when you start videotaping a child, and he or she goes crazy for a minute. However, I never noticed how much people would change when they got in front of the camera, until I stepped into a bit of the spotlight myself.

While I was definitely nervous the first few times I was filmed, I was always just being me—and apparently, that's a rarity. Being self-deprecating and able to recognize my own flaws were attributes that viewers appreciated.

People thanked me for shrugging my shoulders and laughing when my three-year-old son peed on Adrienne Maloof's lawn. I didn't think I was doing anything groundbreaking. I had a little boy I was still potty training, and he had the decency to get out of the pool to pee. What kind of mother would I be if I punished him for (a) not going to the bathroom in his pants and (b) knowing that proper etiquette is to remove yourself from the pool before urinating? I consider that a win. Mothers can feign shock all they want, but please don't act as if in a pinch you've never told your kids to pee behind a tree.

The show became a megaphone for my filter-free, oftentimes crass commentary. I was never the kind of girl to fake it—not for a man (well, maybe a couple of times) and definitely not for a camera. Whom would that serve? Can you imagine how boring a proper, buttoned-up Brandi in a one-piece bathing suit would be? Never going to happen. Ever.

I'm not everyone's cup of tea, but that's the great part: I don't have to be. You don't have to like me, but you damn well know whatever is coming out of my mouth is what I believe the truth to be (poor Winston Churchill). I learned a lot of lessons over the past few years, and I've found that honesty is always the best policy. Lying only gets you more lying—and mounting lies only lead to stress. And stress can lead to premature aging and oftentimes depression. I have my Lexapro, so I'm pretty much just worried about the wrinkles.

It's true Los Angeles doesn't have actual seasons, but for a week or so in late September, you start to notice the days getting shorter and the night air getting a bit cooler. Autumn is quickly approaching.

One autumn evening, I peered out the window to check on Mason and Jake, who were playing in the backyard, and stopped to gaze at the pink sky. The sun was setting, and my canyon home had a perfect western exposure. I grabbed a glass of wine and my iPad and headed out back. The boys were on the swings laughing hysterically as Chica and Sugar jumped at their feet. I clicked on the iPad and went to Google. I decided to type my name into the "news" tab and see what popped up. I started scrolling through a list of stories about the upcoming season of *Housewives*, a press release about my upcoming book, and a few photos of me promoting my new dress line. It took a minute for it to register, but to my utter amazement, there was not one mention of my ex-husband or his new wife. I put the iPad down and took a moment to appreciate what had just happened.

It was official. I had moved on.

ACKNOWLEDGMENTS

I would like to thank my ex-husband, Edward Cibrian, for giving me all the material I could ever need to write this book and for helping me discover the strong independent woman inside of me.

I want to thank my dear friend and boss, Alex Baskin, for believing in me and fighting for me, even though we have never slept together. Also Jennifer Redinger for helping me through the casting process and rooting for me to get the job.

Thank you to lord of the gays, Andy Cohen. A big fat kiss to Doug Ross, Dave Rupel, and all of Bravo TV and Evolution media. Especially the crew who have spent many long days in my home filming and have become an extension of my family.

To my REAL family, Guy and Judy, thank you for raising me to always fight my own battles and never give up, you both amaze me with every second that passes. Thank you for giving me all the information I needed to make my own decisions and become an individual. I am lucky to have such wonderful parents. To my big sister Tricia and younger brother Michael, thank you for the weirdest and most memorable childhood ever. I mean, the stories we could tell. Those were the days. I love you both, as well as your families. I'm sorry for making you believe that you were adopted and that mom, dad and, I were moving to Spain without you guys—hahahaha.

I want to thank ALL of my BFFs, who in the tough times have become one giant surrogate family to me. Trina Prantil my soul mate, Darin Harvey the best human being I know, Jennifer Gimenez my sister from another mother, Janelle Hallier for being generous to a fault, Masha Chase for loving me even after we argue, Claudia Orellana for having the biggest heart, Adrienne Janic Brutsman for being the most loyal person on the planet, Kristen Taekman for sticking it out through the thick and thin with me, Etirsa Inniss for sharing Trina with me, Leslie Bruce for giving me the BEST advice, Emma Heming Willis for showing me how a lady should act but still being able to go gangster, Aime Satchu for always keeping it sexy, Amanda Gold for keeping in me shape while also acting as my therapist, Cari Lee Sladek for showing me how to have fun again, Geneva Wasserman for always coming through for me, Jezika Adams for being way smarter than me, Hillary Tarpin for standing the test of time, Evelyn Subramaniam for being a ray of sunshine all of the time, Gabriella Threlked, for again keeping it sexy, Kimberly Verbeck for letting me and the boys crash on the couch when we were homeless, Krista Heitkamp for making me realize I shouldn't get bunion surgery, Linda Alibrandi for taking me back. Thank you to Crista Klayman for introducing me to so many of my wonderful friends, Lisa Vanderpump and Ken Todd for inviting me into their family, Yolanda Foster for quickly becoming one of my favorite people, Ryan Basford for introducing me to my "gaygent" Michael Broussard, Michael Meldman for making me feel young and beautiful, Stacey Garza for teaching me how to party, Susan Holmes McKagen for being a total rock star, Dr. Sott

Wang for always taking care of me and the boys, Willow Cobanas for being forever young. Thanks to my best editor in the world, Jeremie Ruby-Strauss, who is extremely smart, handsome, and fit (but also extremely married), as well as his assistant, Heather Hunt; publisher Louise Burke and editor-in-chief Jennifer Bergstrom for believing in me; Sally Franklin, Lisa Litwack, Emily Drum, John Paul Jones, and Jamie Putorti for producing a beautiful package; and Jennifer Robinson, Mary McCue, Natalie Ebel, and Ellen Chan for getting the word out.

I feel blessed to have you all in my life and you make me a better person.